£3

Find A Better Life

Discover what you're missing…

GW00646425

Brian Fitzpatrick

Matador
9 Priory Business Park,
Wistow Road, Kibworth Beauchamp,
Leicestershire. LE8 0RX
Tel: 0116 279 2299
Email: books@troubador.co.uk
Web: www.troubador.co.uk/matador
Twitter: @matadorbooks

ISBN 978 1785891 489

British Library Cataloguing in Publication Data.
A catalogue record for this book is available from the British Library.

Printed and bound by CPI Group (UK) Ltd, Croydon, CR0 4YY
Typeset in 11pt Optima by Troubador Publishing Ltd, Leicester, UK

Matador is an imprint of Troubador Publishing Ltd

For Amy, with love.

*This is my story
and it's your story too.*

Contents

Surprises

Life is full of surprises (as we will see). It's funny how little things can turn out to be quite significant later.

I received a Christmas card in 2006 with a very concise message that I found highly amusing, for some strange reason. It so tickled me I've kept it on display ever since.

Years later, as I was finishing this book, it suddenly occurred to me how well that message described my life in the interim.

What did the card say? Only - 'Get it sorted!'

You will be pleased to learn, I did.

Premise

When we have a clearer idea of what shapes us, our thoughts, feelings and actions, we can try other ways that could be more appropriate and rewarding. The rest of life also makes improved sense, increasing our confidence and helping us to relax which ultimately benefits everyone.

There may be no need to change anything. Just experiencing events as they run their course can acquire a fresh significance.

Success

Welcome aboard as we embark on an expedition that tackles the trickery of life in an attempt to broaden our horizons and lift how we feel. Crucially, this is not a study of *other* people. Yes it involves all of us, but primarily it's about YOU.

No matter how far we travel or how much we experience, the one thing that determines the way we view and respond to everything usually manages to escape our notice unless we take a much closer look in the mirror. The distorting effects of our habitual processing mechanisms are rarely addressed or even considered. No surprise then how our encounters contain a certain, not altogether positive, familiarity as we persistently get sucked in, bogged down and worked up by modern living.

Despite being at the controls of the most sophisticated device known, we live our lives with little understanding of it i.e. ourself. Would you try to fly an aircraft with no training or drive a racing car without adequate preparation? Of course not. Still, we typically wander through our entire existence unacquainted with the workings of the remarkable resource at our disposal. We spend years at schools, colleges, universities and work amassing occasionally used information, yet the subject of greatest relevance to us is seldom taught, or seems pointless to learn. Which is a pity, because understanding ourselves better can make a dramatic difference.

This is the chance to achieve what many dream of - being at the heart of the story, where we *surely* belong. If we face this prospect with courage, honesty and an open mind, our troubles tend to recede and a world of opportunity arises.

The long, careful, non-judgemental look in the mirror I advocate may be the critical ingredient for an enhanced life although I have to be honest here, it was despair and confusion, not courage or anything admirable, that forced me to stop and view myself differently. I wanted success without realising what success actually is. Whatever I achieved didn't please me for long and I eventually tired of the aspirations on offer. As someone dear once said about me, 'Nothing was ever enough.' What I really needed was a coherent outlook in a broader context. This was the catalyst for big breakthroughs, and since then I've learned a lot to my advantage. There are two overriding indicators of this new 'success'. Firstly, my health has improved significantly (until I undertook the daunting challenge of writing this book). Secondly, my greater understanding has made me more relaxed overall and seems to be linked to a kind of deep warm glow. Even though my moods certainly vary, I'm learning to make allowances for their deceptions, and the glow is never far away. Oh and thirdly (nearly forgot), curiously I've managed to help one or two people who have been down for a while to perk up pretty quickly.

Now I'm sharing the key lessons from my exploits, and to that end you are heading out on a rather eventful voyage of self-discovery.

This is not a Science book, it doesn't need to be. It's an overview; a compilation of interrelated snapshots that warns about the unreliability of snapshots. Forget certainty for a while. Don't dwell on any concerns regarding details and specifics, for reasons which should become evident.

It's the process that matters; the words are mainly stepping-stones to a more promising vantage point. Themes will emerge. Expect a fair amount of generalising, simplification, speculation, overlap, repetition, contradiction even, and the odd digression. That's fine; that's life; let it flow; let it unfold. (That ought to get me off the hook nicely and provide some valuable room for manoeuvre). Don't worry about learning, changing or applying anything. If you absorb the message, or it absorbs you, things will change. Sounds good? Sounds easy? We'll see.

Incidentally, this story contains twists along the way that are likely to fly in the face of any premature conclusions. So sit back, take your time and allow yourself to experience the effects of what will be a fairly bumpy ride in places. Follow the sequence of topics for maximum return and don't be *too* surprised if you get all shook up by what I throw at you.... that's the general intention.

Good Luck!

Truth

Before we set off, you ought to find out a bit more about me. Why? Because no matter what is explained to us, the deliverer is interpreting to some extent. Emphasis, selectivity, tone and context are common methods. We are always dealing with a version of the 'truth' from elsewhere, coloured by whoever delivers it and how it is delivered. Most of us don't realise but the information is being affected and we would do well to take this into account.

Next we need to recognise that, from the earliest years, our sponge minds pick up ways of assessing, thinking and doing which often persist throughout adulthood. Some are useful, others hold us back. Prejudice (pre-judging) is one example of the latter. We usually come from a preconditioned view and gather what suits from around us to justify it. We don't appreciate we are doing this of course, or the consequent self-imposed restrictions it brings. As we are used to seeing and doing things this way, it is familiar and therefore comfortable somehow, even when it may be harming us. We then pass-on our slanted views, gravitate towards those who predominantly reflect them, and avoid or condemn those who don't. It reminds me of -

The salesman who boasted about having twenty years experience, until his manager pointed out he had merely re-used one year's experience twenty times.

We have all formed agendas that shape our behaviour, many of which remain buried and a mystery even to ourselves. These influence what we acknowledge and feel. We see what we *want* to see, or are used to seeing, wherever possible. Consider opposing supporters describing the same contest, and that says it all. It takes a mountain of reason to overcome a trace of emotion in us, whereas the slightest feeling can be enough to bypass all the evidence in the world. (Emotional resistance to specific considerations often indicates where our greatest gains lie.) The 'truth' is, emotions virtually dictate our so called 'reasoning'.

Being human I'm no different in these respects, suggesting my views could be skewed, flawed or mood prone in places. (If you were looking for certainty, welcome to the *real* world.) So it will help if we drop in some background about me as we go along. For now, here is a brief synopsis indicating what flavours my distinct take on reality.

The eldest of three children, I was raised in a down to earth urban environment by volatile parents. My relationship with them was demanding and lacked intimacy. They did their best and there were many moments of hilarity, though it was far from an ideal upbringing. This probably made me a 'fixer' and dubious about authority. I'm no angry rebel (most of the time), just not particularly impressionable. In the circumstances, understandably, I became anxious but was fortunate to be fairly capable. Thankfully my grandmother provided cherished camaraderie, if not quite full-on affection.

I attended an exceptionally cosmopolitan, non-denominational junior school which made me entirely comfortable with a diverse range of companions. Consequently, I am continually bemused and dismayed by negative views based on superficial generalisations. (The value of mixing children at an early age is enormous.) My later education, at a boys only school, was good for the time. The gender separation worked well for me at that stage despite, or possibly because of, my growing interest in girls.

Then I fell into suitable work which led me to business consultancy, as befitting a 'fixer'. Perhaps my experience in fact finding, problem solving and reporting forms a large part of what I bring to the exploration of life issues. From business improvement to life improvement is a reasonably organic progression. However, practising the elusive art of fluid concepts that can be more beneficial than hard 'facts', has proved a testing departure.

I never invested fully in anything for very long. To complicate matters, musical aspirations would surface from time to time preventing my feet from truly touching the ground. I suppose I was still searching.

That's enough of a backdrop for now but don't fret, we'll glance again at my riveting past shortly. Just bear in mind - if my 'fixer' tendencies give the impression life is a problem to be solved, it isn't. Life is an opportunity to be relished. How we consistently manage to miss this is the intriguing question.

What's Going On

We are entangled in a window-dressed, synthetic, inadequate 'reality'. It modifies us and feeds itself from the false needs produced. This incomplete situation is high-maintenance, with a few advantages and several drawbacks. It generally fails to satisfy, unless we become more aware of our individual contribution to the mix-up.

LOST

There's more to us than we realise because modern living isn't tuned in to vital aspects of our functioning. The card game of life has dealt us a hand which we blindly play without knowing the game or even looking at our cards. When the lights come on, what we previously admired, dismissed or took for granted could appear very different.

Appreciating how lost we actually are, and why our escalating agitation doesn't help, is an important first step towards finding better ways.

Winning

I once read about a Psychologist whose patient said despairingly, 'Sometimes I don't feel part of the human race.' The Psychologist replied, 'Some day you might win the race.'

'What on earth does that mean?' I thought sceptically.

Now I know!

I'm not saying life is a race, that's a costly popular misconception. Life is a fascinating adventure that has us baffled from the outset. It remains a mystery as we charge around in vain or resign ourselves to fate. Early influences predispose us to getting lost, and typically that's what happens. Largely because much of our world has been shaped by people attempting 'improvement' using a basic palette; strong instincts to follow and copy have led us straight into their maze.

Then there is our inherent anxiety. It has probably been a powerful driver, propelling us to the forefront of species rather rapidly, if uncomfortably. The accelerated 'progress' it creates is one way to live although unchecked it contains the potential source of it's own demise, along with a fair dose of on-going dissatisfaction.

Lost and worried doesn't sound like the perfect basis for living, and it's not. The suffering, monotony and misery we manage to create and endure is testimony to that. Fortunately it's not the full story. We have the capacity to deal with these adverse issues, rather than continuing to dance around them. Better judgement based on more complete concepts is what delivers improved results. As a hunter tracks prey, or a scientist tests a theory, skilful determination to follow the abundant evidence we usually ignore pays dividends.

Make no mistake, this is a contest. A contest we either win or lose as individuals. It can only be resolved in our own minds by examining –

1. *What we have simply inherited or absorbed, and what we have personally figured out.*

2. *What we are, as opposed to what we assume we are.*

Guidance surround us, masked by the distracting products of our attempts to get by till now.

Being lost and afraid is so ingrained, our lives as well as our societies have come to rely on it. That's the irony. We are not about to disown or even expose what torments us without a struggle, when we have fashioned ourselves around it almost entirely.

Confronting our fears and confusion may be a tall order but it looks like the only way through… or could it be more interesting than that?

Memories

Back to me again as promised, this time for a very pertinent illustration.

My earliest memory is of impressing my mother and grandmother with an exhibition of exceptional driving skill in a 'Baby-walker' device somewhere around the age of 6 or 7 months, as I recall. They dangled me in this framed contraption with wheels, which I enthusiastically lined up, preparing to dive through a door space not much wider than my vehicle. After a bold run-up of a few yards (or metres nowadays), I lifted my feet and slipped through at speed without touching the tight doorframe, to the rapturous applause of my 'pretending to be amazed' audience (I had a lot to learn about female tactics, and still do). It was a long haul back for the next exhibition of my deft skills, and I was all too willing to oblige my fans as long as their cheers came on cue. On reflection, my infant accomplishments were no mean feat, especially for a child with undetected severe myopia. Alas however, we're not here to drool over my indisputable baby-driver prowess.

Impressed as you no doubt are by my remarkable exploits, I can tell you remain somewhat perplexed as to their connection with life enhancing revelations. Well think back because I and probably you too, have lived the bulk of our lives based on such early formative experiences.

Repeatedly I've tried to run before I could walk. I have chased recognition by carefully calculated and dispatched demonstrations of my modest abilities, oblivious to the burdens this placed on me. Like any child, my thrills only lasted a while. I didn't know what to do next so I took a break and tried again...and again...and again... phew! Nobody told me when it was time to grow up.

What have *you* been doing over and over again throughout your life, in various forms, to get what you liked or to avoid what you disliked when you were a child? Now listen to me –

It's all nonsense!

You don't need that any more!

It's time to grow up!

Other early memories such as child perceptions of 'abandonment' have also controlled me without my knowledge. I became 'tough' to hide that fear, mainly from myself, and most of us are unwitting masters of comparable personal cover-ups. We can't change overnight but we can shed some light on our obsolete motivations and influences, to reduce their hold. Hopefully the lessons I have learned will help you but beware, help can make us lazy. I can't take a single step for anyone on their self-discovery adventure. No one can. It's a very personal expedition.

Not Growing Up

One point I will be emphasising is that we are designed to grow up although you, me and almost everyone else fails to do so adequately, to our detriment. Child thinking in adult bodies is our pervasive modern impediment. As children, we mostly deal in how things appear or have been conveyed to us by others. Children make all sorts of false assumptions based on appearances. (Find out about this if you like – read the Psychology, it's fascinating and amusing.) As we grow, we gradually come to suspect that things might not be quite so cut and dried. Then our next hiccup occurs. Blissfully unaware, we get diverted straight onto a routine path designed by our society which is yet again full of judgements based on appearances and labels. This leaves us vulnerable and poorly prepared for life. Consequently, in adulthood we can feel lost or extremely upset when faced with setbacks, and expect to be rescued – yes, just like children. We haven't been told much about the deceptive nature of appearances or the value of growing up.

Ancient cultures performed coming of age rituals and ceremonies. Examples appear in Mythology, and they would doubtless have been necessary for the survival and development of our earliest ancestors long before records even existed. They included being 'thrown in at the deep end' and forced to 'swim for safety', or being sent on 'long arduous journeys to find and bring back something elusive'. These are metaphors for engaging with life. We retain certain age-related ceremonies for conformity and social purposes without much of the precious growing up lessons or lifestyle changes being passed on. We have forgotten the point, become complacent and let things slip.

Like our ancestors, if we're looking for better lives we need to grow up, whatever that entails? We have to see what has happened to us and learn to appropriately manage ourselves, our responsibilities and concerns. Anyone who finds the sound of this uncomfortable is in child mode, and that covers the overwhelming majority of us. The good news is, we are equipped to grow up and that is how we thrive.

I managed to avoid growing up for many years and could never be described as sheltered or privileged by modern standards. I eventually stumbled upon the benefits when all else failed. My combination of trial and error, being a bit of a free spirit and not settling for what seemed to be the norm for very long has cost me dearly at times. No matter what, the resultant rewards of experiencing what growing up brings have been well worth it.

Nonsense

How *do* we find better ways then? Well, it helps if we have had enough. Enough running around searching for something elusive. Enough waiting for 'more' to come along. Enough showing off, arguing, complaining, doom and gloom. Enough chasing money, status or fleeting excitement. Enough searching for love or anything that temporarily fills the gaps. Our energy is drained by this type of nonsense. I don't mean fun nonsense, a bit of fun is fine by me. I mean ridiculous everyday nonsense. Nonsense at work, nonsense in relationships, nonsense in the media. We are surrounded by lost people with agendas, spouting abundant nonsense, professing to show us what our lives should be about. (Just like me? Fair comment, though I would reserve judgement on that if I were you.) Somewhere among all this, most of us plod wearily through a roller-coaster existence until we run out of steam. Is this it? Surely that isn't all there is?

Alternatively, if you think we're doing ok that's super. Splendid! I'm pleased. You must be one of the lucky few. If it's not broken don't fix it, that's my view.

For those who *are* interested, my job is to explain we can do far better. If the exploration this involves is enjoyable, leads to less difficulties and improves how we feel at the same time, then why not give it a shot?

Don't get me wrong, I'm not preaching or complaining. Oh no, I'm just doing my best to help. I'm comfortable, appreciative and enthusiastic as never before. I work around the nonsense where necessary. After a life spent searching, I see through the pointlessness. I refuse to get dragged into it, and intend to do what I can to expose the high price we pay for our participation. That suits me for now.

So *why* do our lives contain all this nonsense, fuss and drama when human insignificance is clear to a blind man? Our lifespan may seem lengthy to us whereas it is a mere blink of an eye when compared to the millions and billions of years that elapsed before we got here, and will continue to elapse long after we are gone and forgotten. Our achievements and influence may look important until we view our diminutive scale of operation against the vast backdrop of infinite outer-space. If our planet blew up tomorrow, as planets often do, what difference would it make in the grand scheme of things? None, of course. On this basis nothing really matters that much, yet we persist in dramas that damage one another, in tit for tat feuds worthy of the most self-centred children. Why?

We are deluded, that's why, partly because we don't see the bigger picture and partly because we don't *want* to see a bigger picture. In our delusion, controversy and drama are some of the commonest devices we use to dodge our demons or fabricate importance where little exists. They produce a kind of smoke screen, or perhaps 'fog' better describes the blind anxious bumping into each other that arises. For survival reasons, 'insignificant' is the last word children want to apply to themselves. Adults, on the other hand, should know better but we don't at the moment. Like children, we use distracting dramas to gain attention and create social or media interest, till they end up taking us over.

Then we have group dramas where our demands for significance take us into some readily available social, political or religious offer of reward for service. (These often represent the scope of our limited 'big picture'.) We continue to fall for one of the oldest manipulating tricks in the book, designed to provide a sense of importance and belonging by making us part of some established grouping. They usually arouse regressive aspects of our primal tribal instincts. The more insecure and 'underdeveloped' we are, the greater their appeal. I'm not only referring to extremists and fanatics. No, this is about you and me and our questionable allegiances. We are easily influenced, particularly by authority figures in childhood. Prisoners want to be free but our conditioning prison is far more effective because we rarely detect it, so we don't realise we need out. Our awareness and thoughts are being suppressed, which creates pressure inside us. In severe cases we seek outlets or targets to release the pressure (opponents and enemies), recriminations then follow taking us deeper into the mire.

Rather than using our potential constructively, the way we live now contributes to us regularly cancelling out one another as we attempt to conjure up superior personal significance from meagre evidence. Avoiding what we are (or are not) is futile and exhausting. Who knows, if we stopped this nonsense it could be enlightening.

'That's all very well,' I hear you say. 'But how can our lives benefit from reflecting on some bigger picture that incorporates squillions of miles or years, when our attention is required here and now?'… and I would agree, up to a point. That said; where it is elementary and harmless to give our attention to the present in a larger context, we *may* be led to an improved sense of proportion and consequently, fresh perspectives. These in turn save us from covering the same ground endlessly, and perhaps create helpful new possibilities. In other words, utilising the full extent of our personal vision rather than limiting it with traditional ideas and approaches is likely to be in everyone's interest, as we will hopefully determine. Hallelujah!

Progress?

We spend our lives wanting to be what we are not, largely because we haven't sufficiently embraced what we actually are.

Most things are built for situations and purposes – animals, plants, machines *and* humans. They deteriorate, malfunction or require substantial maintenance if they are misused or unsuitably located. Our organic adaptation mechanisms can't handle the type and scale of operating changes we sometimes attempt. In other cases they require considerably more time than we provide to accommodate change.

Natural circumstances are what we now prefer for most living things wherever practicable, without acknowledging modern life and work for humans is mainly at odds with our nature. We passionately condemn the confinement of animals, while human confinement in contemporary societies is rapidly increasing. The resulting intensity of ever more congested surroundings places heavy demands on our tolerance and social abilities.

Physical and mental constraints go hand in hand, so congestion also contributes to stifled perspectives. Many of us voluntarily spend our lives in houses, offices, shops, pubs, clubs, gyms, cinemas and cars. We are glued to computers, mobile phones and TV screens for much of the day and often consider it enjoyment. This has social and health consequences because it is far removed from our predetermined functionality. What has happened?

Past

When we began settling down to become farmers around ten thousand years ago, it seemed like a good idea at the time. However, there *were* trade-offs. Countless years spent roaming and living from hand to mouth had created a resilient resourceful species (I expect) whose emphasis was about to change. Enormous benefits have accrued without us necessarily feeling good overall about our 'improved' circumstances – 'All that glitters isn't gold.'

Ten thousand years isn't very long in Nature's terms. Remember, that was only the beginning of settling and it took many of us longer to succumb. In other words, this is a relatively recent human alteration. It's an alteration we don't fully understand, one we haven't completely adapted to and possibly never will.

Human design is the refined product of related earlier species flowing with, and making use of, changing environments over many millions of years. Our bodies, senses and emotions were all finely tuned to dealing with this in a variety of ways at a suitable pace. The territories we roamed on foot for threats and opportunities were more varied and arduous than our prescriptive modern lifestyles ordinarily entail. It was challenging, and it shaped us accordingly.

Settling, farming and the range of other work it enabled were no soft options though. They had their demands, especially before automation reduced labour intensiveness dramatically. The underlying complication remains that we were not formed by raising and managing animals or crops in relatively tight areas for our convenience. We may have risen to these new tests, and they have yielded returns, but what is this arrangement doing to us?

Present

Nearly three hundred years ago David Hume, one of the fathers of our prevailing economic model, said something like, 'It makes a man as stupid as it is possible to be.' This was probably because our system focuses us on specific, often repetitive, tasks in order to maximise efficiency. Public libraries were supposedly introduced to help counter the stifling effects, without much general success. We now mostly find ourselves underdeveloped individuals, as a result of such narrow conditioning and failure to recognise it, let alone compensate. Our balance has been distorted by repetition and niche operating. Concentration on set sectors of work may lead to certain expertise and perhaps higher throughput, without necessarily providing the variety and stimulation we require.

Hunting and exploring (in it's widest sense) are the core activities that moulded humans. Nowadays, work is described as man's modern version of hunting but they could hardly be farther apart. It will be interesting to see what form we derive from modern work and lifestyles, if they don't strain and weaken us irrevocably.

Modern work is saturated with restrictive regulation and conformity. Increased automation, fewer outdoor tasks, repetition and less varied physical requirements all conspire against our innate functioning. Large-scale organising structures find it hard to allow for individuality and can be cumbersome to adapt. Working practices have swung towards greater comfort, control and detail which may seem desirable but these developments reduce personal resourcefulness while increasing weakness, dependency and obsessiveness, which are becoming widespread.

Neither our inherent make-up nor our progress in knowledge, civilisation and sophistication are adequately reflected in modern societies and the blinkered models for living they adopt. Consequently, we have exhausted our current approaches and are ready for new routes with the motivation they bring. (Even if many of us are too preoccupied with our heads down to see this, despite suffering the damaging by-products of modern constraints.)

We're not only square pegs in round holes, as societies we pander to regressive tendencies that mushroom where uninspiring routines prevail. Modern mass culture continually triggers the least developed aspects of our character. We are easily lured into the shallows by celebrities, status, gadgets and a range of childish entertainment topics from wizards, super-heroes and animated fantasy; to sci-fi, romance, sport and soap operas. Reworked variations on tired themes are commonplace. No wonder we get despondent and frustrated.

Confinement and forced adaptation are short-sighted tactics. Perhaps this was the best we could do a few hundred years ago to create the necessary circumstances for us to move on, however it is now time to do so.

Future

This is not about blame. That would be to miss the wider point and our common responsibilities. Numerous systems have been tried over the years and, in spite of their drawbacks, we have plenty to thank them for.

Now it is up to us, the latest generations, to refine the present and shape a fitting future. Success depends on a constructive commitment to this and minimising complacency.

Distractions

The modern aspirations we have been offered to relieve our frustrations usually deliver temporary respite only, and further fuzz our accelerating restless mindsets. We can be easily distracted, and the modern world is full of distractions which are regularly portrayed as what life is all about. They include gadgets, travel, entertainment, furnishings, clothes, partners, cars and every other advertisers dream. As well as these, Nature's distractions such as sexual attraction are overstimulated in larger communities, and by media exposure. Add alcohol, the internet, gambling, drugs and you have a potent cocktail. The thing is, these are so widely used, few people realise they are distractions. Distractions from what? In moderation distractions are harmless and enjoyable, as a life focus they leave a lot to be desired.

Agitated minds often gravitate towards distractions in their need to fill the gaps created by their runaway mental appetites. Glamorised portrayals of life centre around distractions, and the child in us is attracted to their surface appeal as conveyed by the highly selective media. We conveniently disregard the numerous celebrity casualties or what lies behind the scenes, as this requires us to entirely reassess our superficial view of the world.

A child is readily distracted by new or attractive things but for our stability, and if we are to be productive responsible members of the society which supports us, we have to manage our appetite for distractions. Insecurity, limited willpower or a lack of any meaningful purpose can make this difficult. When work and lifestyles are seen as routine or.dull, distractions offer a temporary buzz or escape. This is the self-perpetuating work/play trap that leaves little room for growth. It's our take on a crude public order device that's been around for centuries. The ancient Romans referred to it as 'bread and circuses for the masses'. As distractions need to be continually topped-up, many people get locked into this cycle and are damaged physically or psychologically or both. This has considerable negative spin-off effects on society as a whole, including a fair share of the enormous effort we put into healthcare and dealing with crime. We could call it waste but that would be an oversimplification.

Spectating

We can learn by watching. Looking on as our children play, or taking in an open landscape can be heart warming. Watching can also provide a healthy release or social opportunity. Having said all that, watching in place of participating has now reached epidemic proportions. Thousands of adults frequently flocking to see entertainers or figureheads, and becoming personally identified with their performance or proclamations, is a diversion from our requisite input to life. Moreover, the watchers' feelings ordinarily hinge on what they witness.

Mass media like television and the internet take distraction and spectating life decay to another level. We drop from at least being present, to absent and remote. There is no need for full social interaction or even to leave our sofa. We can edit what we watch, hear or read, and vet other participants (if any) to maintain our comfort zones and reinforce preset prejudices. We are digging a hole for ourselves that just keeps getting deeper.

Towns & Cities

Aside from the advantages, we have our work cut out for us operating in close proximity to numerous strangers in busy urban settings. We may not appreciate it but this takes it's toll. For all our concerns about natural habitats, we ignore that cities are entirely man-made and unnatural for us, no matter how many contrived parks, trees or flower borders we install.

Epidemics, spreading quickly in large close communities, are notorious for decimating populations. We have taken many steps to reduce the risks, such as healthcare, improved sanitation and prompt containment where possible. Still, large cities remain breeding grounds for major infections.

The faster pace and greater anxiety caused by population congestion puts pressure on us that leads to ill health and friction. We are sponges and comparison machines, absorbing and processing what is around us automatically. The problem is, like any machine, we have a limited capacity. When our capacity is exhausted our functioning is impaired, cracks appear and ultimately something has to give.

In larger communities, and increasingly through the media in more remote communities, we are constantly bombarded with messages and choices that have become so familiar their mental processing demands go unnoticed. Listening to talking speeds we notice how they are rising, along with speech volumes which climb in order to be heard above the competition. All of this feeds stress and strain.

In a city we are surrounded by strangers and this is a lot of work. What are they like? How do we pass politely and efficiently? Add city shopping, navigation, reading signs, music, traffic, advertising, and now our mind is in overdrive. To the 'overstimulated' mind this feels merely routine but it is draining.

Our mind sees every new situation as a threat, an opportunity or neutral, and unfamiliar encounters are routinely assessed for this. Busy environments force us to accelerate or avoid assessing by using shortcuts and barriers. Relationships with our fellow humans suffer as a result. The forced barriers and indifference to others we create for 'efficiency and protection' are counterproductive and self-perpetuating. They lead to alienation from our neighbours rather than improving our abilities to live together. Superficial cooperation may be achieved without the natural caring and sharing which contributes to our overall welfare. (Apparently communities who care about, and mix well with, their neighbours live far longer.)

If we fail to mix appropriately, we lose valuable social skills and benefits. Our ability to mix is then impaired further, we get more isolated and eventually critical and/or fearful of others. Camps emerge and philosophical or physical attacks are interspersed with a restless peace. Bullies or pressure groups often exploit this lack of social cohesion. Divide and conquer is their goal, where all they really need to do is intimidate. The necessary division is conveniently provided by a climate of fear and mistrust caused by the alienating effects of our acquired social barriers. In better connected societies, these opportunists could not thrive and would be less liable to appear.

Human opportunism is natural and healthy to a degree. It keeps us on our toes. However, bullying and exploitation create escalating dangers for all parties.

Cooperation

Humans have never been the fastest, strongest or most robust of species, yet we have grown to dominate our predators and the world as we know it in a relatively short time. This is no fluke. It owes a great deal to our cooperative social tendencies, tied in with a bit of appropriate competition. We have a range of individual abilities and are capable of combining these in a wide variety of ways. (Theories suggest our large brains may be partly due to this.) Cooperation is fundamental to us. You can see it when the chips are down. Our natural caring sharing mechanisms kick in when things get tough, as in times of war, illness or loss. Throughout Nature, flocks of birds, herds of animals, shoals of fish and swarms of insects instinctively come together using their own bonding systems to create a whole greater than the sum of their parts, that operates as a single entity when necessary. Human cooperation is usually a more conscious device that may not quite have the same cohesive approach but it too can be highly effective.

We have used cooperation to do some of our best work in the past, and modern complex societies are entirely based upon it. Although we change through time, our current lifestyles require considerable cooperative interaction with other humans. It seems 100 to 150 people may be our optimum level for now, which is probably a product of historically viable family/tribal numbers. This indicates that a pivotal part of our happiness and healthy functioning could be to know, mix and cooperate with roughly this amount of people (not all the time or all at once).

Perhaps now we can begin to see the disadvantages of social withdrawal, barriers and division. We are not cut out to flourish this way. These questionable features hint at detrimental early conditioning being exacerbated by clouded mindsets. The ensuing lack of involvement results in a wealth of lost opportunities... to put it mildly.

Leaders

It is also fair to say we 'cooperate' in groups to *attack* other groups or individuals. Underlying this is often fear, prejudice and a fair measure of suspect leadership.

Our primal pack instincts predispose us to following leaders at times, so our leadership choices are important. This is tricky without a clearer idea of what drives us, and leadership figures in particular. Masking insecurity, and the need for recognition often creates leadership aspirations. Various circumstances can bring extreme types of these personalities to the fore, and history is full of destructive examples. They pander to our concerns, look the part or talk a good game, which makes them superficially attractive, like many of our choices in life.

Healthy progress requires leaders to encourage self-leadership, as a wise father would. Leaders who strive for and cling to power give the opposite signals, hindering us all.

As we traditionally harbour 'them and us' attitudes, our world contains it's fair share of leaders who reflect these to an extent. Consider how we are surrounded by subtle, and not so subtle, nationalism throughout our lives – from selective versions of history at school to loaded movie themes and regular reporting of national 'heroes' or events. If all countries adopt the same approach (as they mainly do) it is hardly surprising that feelings of suspicion, hostility and fear between nations, groups and individuals are fostered. Living constantly in a world of 'them and us' is hard work because even subtle threats require us to have our defence mechanisms on standby. This limits our ability to relax, affecting our health and happiness, while making the world seem unduly forbidding. Crazy? Of course it is, but that's what happens when we remain like insecure children grasping at convenient illusions in our relentless pursuit of personal validation.

In modern large societies, improved integration requires better understanding. Prescribed tolerance is not sustainable and won't deliver genuine benefits without careful examination of our barriers. So why *do* we alienate ourselves from others? There are a multitude of reasons, some justifiable to a degree although conditioning has a lot to answer for. Our part in shaping the world and the responses of people around us has more to do with our influenced attitudes and behaviour than we admit. We have a tendency to make life awkward for ourselves by failing to spot our obsolete programming.

Given all this, it is not surprising that progress is erratic and fragile, not to say seriously volatile at times. If we continue making choices with limited insight we will pay the price. Until we learn more about our conditioned reasoning, and dig beneath propaganda and superficial representations, we are unlikely to choose the best leaders (or anything else) because we can be so readily mis led.

Obsessive

I saw a young Beagle on TV sniffing the ground till it's nose bled. Apparently the problem was down to a lack of varied walks and inadequate use of it's Beagle instincts. The injurious obsessive behaviour was caused by unsuitable restrictions, and most of us live our own versions.

Caged or otherwise constrained animals become obsessive. They start repeating actions over and over, eventually causing themselves physical harm. Their minds and bodies are not operating as intended so essentially they are 'imploding'. They're instinctively trying to push forward, with few satisfactory outlets. We humans do likewise. Our big brains are currently struggling to cope with self-imposed physical and mental confinement. Confinement combined with overstimulation means we find it difficult to unwind. When we always have to be doing something, the ravaging fire is continually stoked. Never at peace and all the worse for it. Numerous things suffer, including our health, as anxiety and obsessive behaviour take hold. (I was about to say it doesn't get much more obsessive than writing books like this but sadly, it does.)

Obsessiveness creates mountains out of molehills and exaggerated grievances – the postman not closing the gate, the noise of a dog barking or children playing. Fussing over clothes, people's actions and news stories is increasingly commonplace. Over and above that – examples of weird human activities abound, particularly in large cities, caused by a lack of sufficient purpose. As for our more mainstream pursuits – stamp collecting, train spotting and hoarding obscure memorabilia may seem slightly odd but what about the vast wine collections, car fleets or animal menageries some accumulate.

People pay fortunes for jewels, paintings and antiques whose perceived value is status enhancement or investment potential. In this curious supply and demand game of pass the parcel, historical significance, rarity, or being the product of exceptional human skill are a few of the dubious justifications given for sky-high prices. Nonetheless, I suspect you will resist my comments as they contradict our entire world view of what is precious. A true story with stirring implications might help...

One morning I had a feeling I was about to meet someone significant that day. I went to a nearby museum where I enjoy walking through the grounds. The buildings are pleasant and the art is interesting but they seem staid by comparison to the natural surroundings with their array of plant and bird life, constant changes, sounds, smells, colours and feel. As I passed the main door during my walk outside, an elderly lady emerged from the building alone. There was no-one else to be seen. She stopped in front of me, looked back at the museum and said, 'I much prefer what is out here to what is in there.' (I don't think she meant me). I smiled. She got it. You don't come across people with that insight every day. Was this the meeting I had anticipated?

Food Glorious Food?

We need food to live, it forms a large part of our lives. It also accounts for a large part of our bodies, larger than many of us would like. Recent attitudes to food illustrate how obsessive our narrow lives have become. Food is simply fuel, although we now seem to possess an abundance of time to analyse and play with it. Food is certainly necessary, care is wise and there are always improvements to be made. Appreciating and savouring our food is important too, but – fine dining, ceaselessly counting calories and checking ingredients, watching TV chefs or cooking competitions, and never-ending recipes, all point to us being people with little of any real significance on our plates. What do many of us do when we are at a loose end? Yes, we eat or drink. We get overweight and sick. We diet, we binge, we use 'treats' to placate our children and food or drink to cover our emotional problems. It all amounts to applying readily available substitutes as compensation for something more elusive. Food is another distraction to fill the gaps; an easy temporary escape from lives lacking substance, or a 'serious threat' to be constantly kept in check.

Living In A Box

A prime contributor to our obsessiveness, disguised by it's familiarity and convenience, is living indoors. We return to the same house, in the same street, in the same town for years on end. Looking down from an aeroplane we think, 'Do I really live in one of those boxes?' Of course we do. We must adorn and attend to our boxes frequently if they are to be adequately maintained. They are usually our largest financial investment. Houses can do more harm than good although we never consider it because most of us live this way. That's human conditioning for you – everyone does it so it must be ok. (*Hence the story of 'The Emperor's New Clothes'.*)

'We need shelter,' I hear you say. 'We live in a cold climate, it rains or gets too hot.' Admittedly we need shelter but do we *really* need fancy flooring, multiple media gadgets, hi-tech kitchens and bathrooms, bone china dinner sets, elaborate ornaments and fussy cushions? Obviously not, so what's going on and how did we get sucked into all this… stuff?

It was caused by not thinking for ourselves, the cause of many problems. Yes, our house obsession did start with a need for shelter. It is reasonable for the shelter to be pleasant, especially if the climate requires us to use it a lot, so some degree of decoration is worthwhile. Thereafter we have a choice of where to spend our time – inside or outside.

Like outdoor plants, we were shaped by external habitats over aeons. The more we stay indoors the more difficult it gets to face healthy external exposure for any length of time. If the indoor aspects of our environment are developed by us and our community, while the outdoor aspects are not (like toilets, ad-hoc shelters, seating, security and outdoor skills), then we inevitably live more indoors and weaken. Try growing an outdoor plant inside and see what you end up with.

Living indoors turns into another self-perpetuating downward spiral if you let it. Our world gets smaller and tighter. When our world is small we can grow steadily more self-absorbed. Worry, unhappiness and ill health then come knocking. In towns and cities it is more manageable to have people indoors but it is unlikely to be healthier overall.

Furthermore, being housed close to many others who are virtual strangers puts our natural comparing survival instincts into overdrive, together with various inherent territorial and congestion reactions. We then obsess about boundaries, neighbours, walls, gardens, or noise, and become prone to physical as well as mental ailments because we are not equipped for so much of this nonsense.

We can see our true outdoor nature as soon as fair weather arrives; people flock to outdoor cafés, bars, barbecues, parks and beaches. Some of us enjoy walking, climbing, sailing and other external activities. However, due to the damage already done by confined lifestyles, these ventures often reflect obsessive behaviour simply transferred to an outside setting. At one end of the spectrum we see a frustration reaction to our confinement in frenetic enthusiasm as we attempt the – highest, fastest, toughest, coldest, hottest, longest, mostest and so on. At the other extreme we display a type of fatalistic surrender to the habits of restriction by following familiar or prescribed routes and routines outdoors with the usual companions.

We rarely connect with the Nature that formed us, as advantageously as we could do.

Addiction

You probably expect me to rant on about drugs or alcohol. You may have a particular interest in this or say, 'It doesn't apply to me.' But I'm not, and it *does* apply to you. Those addictions are just the tip of the iceberg, the ones we can see, the acknowledged ones. I'm talking about habits, the unseen addictions we have all succumbed to from living contained lives. Our daily rituals and regimes, people and places we frequent, media habits, interests and beliefs, all go unnoticed as key factors limiting our outlook and development. Most of us are addicts and although some of our habits can be useful, their hold is generally excessive.

A friend once told me, 'It's easy to quit smoking, I've done it hundreds of times.' If you really want to see the extent of our addictions stop using your mobile phone or computer, watching televison, reading magazines or newspapers, listening to music or the radio, buying stuff, running around, drinking tea or coffee, being with other people. How long can you last? Feel the acute withdrawal symptoms when you try. That's what I call 'addiction' – something we can't stop for long, or that craves to be replaced as soon as possible. This illustrates the unsettled condition of our minds and their desperation for the next fix. Our brains can form channels or grooves from repetitive behaviour and like hidden trenches, we readily fall into them. The bigger they get the harder it is to climb out.

Projecting

Our minds create other complications as we make all kinds of mistakes by over-employing one of our most notable, though unreliable, mental abilities – projecting into the past and future. (There are witty books by specialists explaining the strange mistakes our minds make, especially when projecting.)

When we project, the past is seen in edited highlights or low-lights, overlaid with our current mood and perhaps some recent experience. We have a tendency to add what 'suits' us and remove what doesn't. Emphasis is also distorted and we focus on specific parts taken out of context. As for the future, it is a complete mystery so we select from the present and combine it with our distorted view of the past. This may help us to plan but it's not exactly dependable.

We often prefer to try recreating versions of our mind-distorted past rather than moving forward, which can be more than a little disconcerting when our false past-based expectations of the future fail to materialise, as they often do... unsurprisingly. The fact that we can predict some outcomes with any degree of accuracy is no mean feat, given our susceptibility to falsification when projecting.

A bit of nostalgia or anticipation can be heart-warming, and I'm not saying we shouldn't plan for the future or learn from the past, only that it helps when we recognise the breadth of our mind's erratic creative potential.

To put it bluntly, projecting is riddled with pitfalls.

One typical example of projecting guaranteed to make life tricky is – wrestling with our troubles when we are supposed to be doing something else e.g. sleeping. This increases tension because it's impossible to tackle life's tormentors when we are under the covers (unless they happen to be sharing the bed). In the actual event, our natural present-moment resourcefulness kicks in and things usually fall into place, or not, without the many protracted scenarios we despaired over.

> *'I've lived through some terrible things in my life, some of which actually happened.'*
> MARK TWAIN

I can't count the number of well-meaning people who have

asked me, during the early stages of writing this book, 'So what are you going to do with it when it's finished?' In fact, this is often their first and only question... not, 'How is it coming on?' 'What did you write today?' 'Are you enjoying it?' Nope, it's always about the future and that is frequently caused by an agitated mind. Runaway projecting is a modern widespread habit most of us are completely unaware of.

Unfortunately, when we are confined, underemployed or overstimulated, our big brains tend to project more. To combat the unease this breeds, learning to focus on the present has been the lesson of wise advisers for thousands of years.

The Bogey Man

Allow me to introduce our closest companion. A master of disguise known under many misleading labels such as – bravado, status seeking, jealousy or anger. You may recognise it easier in more obvious forms such as – withdrawal, panic, worry or clinging. It is of course the ultimate four letter word, FEAR.

The close psychological connection between fear and anger has been one of my most illuminating discoveries.

Underlying anxiety and insecurity is rife. The less willing we are to admit it, the more embedded it tends to be and the greater the obstacle it presents to ourselves and those around us. It is a sobering thought to consider that those who we often regard as strong or confident are liable to be hiding serious insecurity, mostly from themselves. The 'confident' swagger and forceful tone are trademark insecurity covers, as are attention-seeking, constant striving and control dramas. The last thing our ego needs is any trace of it's precarious basis, so smoke-screen after smoke-screen is created to avoid detection. Our coping mechanisms will show any face, act any act, at times to hide our vulnerabilities with their obsolete reasons. Fear is our constant stalker from the past that we continually camouflage as adults, until all our strategies are swept aside when some event cuts deep. At this point we meet our 'nemesis' unprepared, and pay the accumulated price of lifelong, unconscious, 'unnecessary' avoidance.

In our hectic modern age, one thing is triggered more than anything and that is fear.

Nothing interests people more than bad news. Perhaps *interests* is the wrong word, *captures* may be more accurate. This makes us sitting ducks for pedlars of panic as they jostle to attract any portion of our daily-diminishing attention spans. The question is, why do we swallow the bait so readily?

If we are to be happier and healthier it helps to consider what creates unhappiness and that has a lot to do with fear. Fear is a vital survival alert apparatus so we are programmed to respond to it promptly and with great attention. Over hundreds of thousands of years living in small groups, we presumably became accustomed to the type and level of threats that related to our survival. Suddenly, in the very recent modern world, we are exposed to the predicaments of vastly increased populations. Our media constantly provides us with (and dramatises) the worst news from billions of other people; our fear impulses go into overdrive and usually stay there. Many of us have learned to 'cope' and don't realise we are being affected, but humans are sponges and negativity is poison to us that can only be handled in low doses. We are not equipped for frequent 'remote' bad news that we cannot attend to, or high levels of negativity. The more exposure we get, the more damage we are likely to incur and the more prone we are to further harm. It's another downward spiral.

Despite the media's apparent vested interest in spreading bad news, they are not at the root of our fear problem. The seeds of recurring fear are sown in early childhood, mainly by anxious parents who create anxious children who become anxious adults and create their own anxious children, and on and on until we acknowledge this. Parts of the personalities adopted by our children and taken into adulthood are often overcompensating for fear, and can appear tough, confident, even 'successful'. Underneath and undetected regularly lies easily triggered anxiety – fear.

One of the most popular phrases we use when parting is, 'Take care.' This habitual expression of concern demonstrates the anxious mindsets we have acquired. Dangers certainly exist, continually reminding each other to be on the lookout for them is hardly reassuring.

'The only thing we have to fear is fear itself.'
PRESIDENT FRANKLIN D. ROOSEVELT

Ego

Like any voyage of discovery, life contains a series of challenges, lessons and rewards. We have now reached the ultimate challenge which yields some of the greatest rewards.

It took a few moments to register fully when a movie character spoke one of the most profound lines I have ever heard – 'Get over yourself!'

It's worth repeating – Get Over Yourself!

I appreciate this may not appear to be the most liberating phrase ever written, so I will try to explain.

Voilà

We don't exist!

I know this sounds shocking and implausible but alas, it is true; which is rather embarrassing when you consider most of our efforts go into confirming and embellishing the significance of our personal existence.

Oh, eh, umm... pity we waste so much time and effort then?

Yep, it sure is!

Self Building

Allow me to elaborate. Something *may* exist (an area we will explore much later) although it is not *us* as we assume we know ourselves. Assuming we know, is the obstacle. Our name, family, age, work, religion, affiliations, nationality and gender are simply standard labels. They say some things about us but mainly overlook our place and functions in any wider context.

I'm choosing the term 'ego' to loosely represent our underlying idea of self we generally take for granted.

The 'false self' we currently presume we are has merely been automatically derived from our surroundings over time, and tweaked using rudimentary data. Not only that, but a great deal of it's basis was concocted in childhood when our minds were far less reliable, and in circumstances which no longer exist. As we grew we forced and squeezed immature ideas of who we were, or wanted to be, to somehow tie in with what was around. Later we selected and moulded what was around us, wherever possible, to fit our picture of the world and 'optimise' our place in it. I expect this has been our life's work for one reason more than any other – our obsolete childhood survival priority legacy. This is compounded in later life by social pressures and the advantage that 'recognition' can bestow on our 'crucial' reproduction chances (even if we're not interested in relationships, sex or children).

Human children are totally reliant on others for a prolonged period, which forms long-term attitudes at this early stage. As children our ego employs a sort of identity to survive and progress in a world which appears fascinating yet puzzling and threatening at times. To have it's needs met, the child usually aims to be at the centre of the view it creates despite any evidence to the contrary, and that is the enormous burden of ego. Egos and identities may help children with their formative minds and needs but a lot of very hard work and much selective reasoning is required to sustain these overstretched fantasies beyond our initial years.

Taking Shape

Genetic characteristics aside, this is my potted version of how we obliviously build and reinforce what we assume we are all about, together with the strategies that accompany it.

If those we rely upon in childhood do not appear to see us as important enough, our survival seems threatened and we must compensate by working harder or cleverer or both, to have our needs met. Crying is the basic technique for babies, which probably turns into complaining or demanding in adulthood if it worked earlier. Children who are unsure of their mother's support will cling rather than explore healthily, setting the stage for a future of abiding insecurity (which often gets masked). As we grow, we construct and adapt a sense of self from whatever obtains the 'necessary' attention. Positive attention is ideal, although negative attention may be preferable to none in the survival game – better to be looked over than overlooked. Essentially, whatever works is used. Afterwards, the mission is to find people and situations that offer variations of what we wanted in childhood.

Alternatively, if children are showered with attention (not necessarily affection), they may feel less need to work at certain things. In fact, in some respects not working can be seen as the thing to do because someone else will 'take care' of us. As we grow (or fail to in this case) we expect to receive from, and be guided by, others. Protection, support and direction are sought from elsewhere, and so we form an identity based on expectations of others. In this scenario authority figures are likely to remain intimidating, and people's opinions can be highly influential. In adulthood we may gravitate towards providers and protectors to supply what we were accustomed to in early life because we have been given little idea of how to fend for ourselves. This unhealthy process also curbs our confidence.

These represent simplified extremes in the creation of our fundamental perspectives. Numerous other aspects and permutations exist, each incorporating natural childhood insecurity fused with a naive view of life and some sort of unbalanced upbringing that moulded most of us. It can be a complex process, well worth reflecting on for clues to our personal make-up. In any case, we are still frantically peddling with our heads down in a dependency based survival race that has long since been overtaken by the subtle onset of adulthood with it's liberating capabilities. The game has changed without us embracing this pivotal alteration.

So the responses we received, along with other early life experiences, provide the basis for our child-constructed ideas of what we are and how we should operate... and these usually stick.

Tactics

A range of devices to meet our ego's 'needs' (which contribute to our behaviour and personality) are constantly tried and tested. Common schemes include drama, boasting, humour, exaggeration, strong image, criticising, chasing wealth or status, bullying, huffs, complaining, generosity, copying, being tough, denying feelings, fitting in, standing out or any amount of combinations. The most effective are re-employed and refined. We rely on their proven 'effectiveness' to obtain the attention, protection, approval or control we craved as children. If they fail, we can be in deep trouble because we have not woken up to the fact that we no longer count on others for our survival. We remain enslaved by a concealed fear that our childhood needs may not be met and these, often convoluted, tactics 'must work or we are doomed'. This is an extremely serious business for our fragile obsolete egos which resemble soldiers cut off in the jungle, still 'dealing with the enemy' years after the war has ended.

Childhood fear-based egos dominate our world at every level and create endless problems, as we adults keep trying to obtain the reassurance we no longer require, and get really upset at the slightest possibility it might not always be available. Continually seeking validation or recognition long after the source of need has gone is our modern, high-maintenance, wild goose chase.

Most of us spend our entire lives ruled by insecure egos and it creates much unnecessary effort and suffering. That is the big lesson. Due to it's flimsy basis, no matter what we achieve, in the background our life, work and relationships can mirror a recurring nightmare we are desperately trying to avoid or distract ourselves from, where something is bound to go horribly wrong at any moment. When difficulties do arise (many of which get no further than our head), the threatening backdrop from childhood soon pops to the fore. The latest concern readily combines with our earliest fears making it feel overpowering. This causes us to overreact, panic or even become traumatised. Now we are in a well-rehearsed drama that confirms our familiar beliefs about life and requires the usual draining strategies. We may be struggling again but familiarity suggests we are right about the world and that is what our fragile ego needs – to be right, and thus reinforced, at any cost.

The trap of ego is we think it's all we are. It seems to be our entire being because we have invested everything in it. To undermine our ego would be like dying so, at every opportunity, we strive to validate the very thing that sabotages our contentment. Repeated toil and trouble is the colossal burden we endure to bolster this shaky fabrication.

Image

Image is another part of the ego's attempts to patch up something from very little. It is a disguise or outfit intended to show ourselves and the world who we think we are and how we want to be perceived. Many of our choices such as relationships, work, interests, tastes and possessions reflect an image. They can say a lot about us. Calm, confusion, agitation and passion are all projected in our choices, that provide more personality indicators than we appreciate. For instance, dogs often reflect what their owners are like or admire. Their appearance or nature may be matching or complementary. Strong, fierce, distinctive, cute, tall and slim, petite and coiffured, rescued, can all tell a tale.

Clothes are like costumes. Some of us dress in bright colours, bold patterns or unusual styles to be noticed, which suggests needy attention-seeking and/or extroversion. Some dress to be invisible, implying withdrawal. Plain coloured, ill fitting or very casual clothes may indicate relaxed indifference, or an 'ambush tactician' whose strategy relies on misleading others – contrived indeed. Very uncoordinated clothing points to a lack of cohesive perspective (or a broken washing machine). Dark colours and smart suits can be based on a need to be taken seriously. Official uniforms like Clergy, Judiciary, Police and Academics are often black for this reason. (A lack of dye options when their traditions originated could be another factor.) Some of us join fashion or anti-fashion groups from a desire to belong, and remain in costume long after the fad has elapsed. The image filled an identity gap in our life which would likely reappear without the 'costume'. Strong personal images are frequently elaborate attempts to obtain the attention, protection or belonging we pursued as children.

All The World's A Stage

Egos can adopt multiple forms to attain their aims. Wide variations in our behaviour show the lengths some of us will go to. We are all actors, playing various parts selected from our repertoire as required in different circumstances. In extreme cases some of us want to become *professional* actors, perhaps for attention, or the 'control' of working to scripts, or possibly because we are confused and have failed to form a satisfactory identity (assuming prescribed roles fills this gap temporarily). The entertainment industry attracts many who seek the type of attention they craved in childhood, and unfortunately this can complicate affairs.

Incidentally, egos are generally attracted to bigger egos in their search for significance, taking us further off course.

Families, work or friends normally supply the stage to perform our misguided personal charades. One hope is that, given enough time and opportunity to act-out childhood notions of what life is about, we will eventually take the first step to a remedy by admitting it doesn't deliver. I say *admit* rather than *realise* because we mostly do realise but see no alternative, so are unlikely to play anything other than our standard roles in the meantime. What else is there?

Self-defeating

In old age and faced with the prospect of his approaching death, a remarkably talented scientist produced a dozen identical copies of himself to confuse the gods. When his time came and the gods arrived to collect him, they were impressed and baffled by his amazing skill. Astutely, one god offered his conditional admiration by saying, 'These are truly wonderful works, alas there is a crucial flaw.' Deeply offended, the scientist stepped forward to demand an explanation. This allowed the wise gods to identify their man and collect him.

Egos are like that, susceptible to the slightest praise or criticism, continually triggering our vanity and insecurities. They are albatrosses round our necks that lead us into all kinds of predicaments and prevent us from growing. They may be hard to shake but until we notice them at least, life remains a threatening struggle when it could be far more gratifying.

Parents

If I had to pick a single factor from all the reasons we become lost it would be our parents, or those responsible for our care in early childhood. The most common reaction to this is dismissal. We may reluctantly accept we look a bit like our parents, yet somehow we are less willing to see how much we think and act like them. Perhaps a healthy rebellious aspect of our nature won't let us concede this. Is it the mists of time or maybe our need for individuality? Some of us are blind, so close we cannot see in this ultimate 'can't (or won't) see the wood for the trees' scenario. For some it is taboo to scrutinise parents. As children we 'deal' with their effects in order to survive, and appear to move on. Part of this involves assuming it is over if it is past but considerable parental influence persists, usually unnoticed. Disregarding all the signs, we pass by the door to the most attainable liberating possibility in our lives without a second glance. Whatever the excuses for detouring, those of us who have been most affected by our parents' particular outlook are often the least likely to consider it.

The reason I stress the importance of parenting is because it lies at the root of all our lives and we can improve it readily. Individual personalities make the world we live in and parents have a lot to do with our personality. They shape us and in turn, we shape the world. If we consider other key factors in personality apart from early upbringing, such as genes and environment – parents have a lot to do with our environment and in most cases they provide our genes, for now. Consequently, parents are an ideal place to investigate for answers.

Accessing this abandoned goldmine requires us to probe popular oversights. When traced thoroughly, we can see that crime, health and our view of the world have much to do with parents. So what underpins the blindness and counterproductive resistance which puts such a persistent obstacle in the way of our improvement? It's a combination of universal circumstances that should be reasonably straightforward to overcome, once acknowledged.

The Need

Human babies are born at a relatively early stage of their development due to various factors. (These include nourishment needs, and the historical complication that our fast expanding brain must come out of the womb before it grows too big to pass through our mother's birth canal.) As we emerge totally helpless, we rely on parents more, and for much longer, than other species. After many months of their close attentions we take our first steps. Following another two years of fairly intensive care and rapid, influence absorbing, brain growth we can just about feed ourselves. By around the age of three we could depend less on parents than we do but modern society rarely requires it. In the event of our parents failing to hinder our progress with their dramas, attentions or neglect, society will ordinarily step in to ensure we remain stuck.

The Players

For their healthy development, children have to feel 'adequately' loved. Apart from the recognised physical aspects, Nature has provided mothers primarily with the emotional equipment and reward mechanisms to nurture babies. If these have been disrupted by the mother's upbringing, her children will no doubt suffer. Our survival strategy is based on obtaining what we require from both parents thus we are also conditioned by our father's input. As with mothers, highly demanding or negligent fathers give rise to damaged children who usually become malfunctioning adults.

Fathers and mothers play complementary roles for children therefore any significant fracture in the parents' relationship, or inconsistent approaches, will confuse or upset their family. Friction and inconsistencies between parents can have serious effects on children's later lives which we fail to take into account sufficiently.

Both parents supply a range of teaching and influences. Broadly speaking, mothers are equipped to offer more emotional assistance while fathers naturally deliver more practicality, part of which can involve preventing mothers from taking their role too far. (There is a fine line between mothering and smothering, as there is between fathering and bullying.) These natural duties have probably worked over thousands of years for good reason and are not easily ignored by recent changes in society. That is not to say there cannot be considerable overlap or role reversal on occasions.

Fathers generally encourage children to be more independent i.e. to 'grow up'. Our current failure to grow up could be described as a fathering deficiency in it's widest sense. What remains of fathering has moved in the mothering direction due to changing times combined with men's modern skewed functioning. Mothering has an important place but ideally both parental aspects require counterbalancing and cross-stimulation by the other. Parental pandering or indifference can lead to a lack of drive in children and failure to inspire their necessary resourcefulness for life's challenges. Balanced parenting sacrifices personal preferences periodically to find the best overall way forward in the longer term. Melodrama, complaining, trivia and expectations of others are on the increase in many modern humans. These are childish traits which a proper fathering influence would discourage in favour of self-development (not self-interest). Discontent is frequently caused by a failure to get the best out of ourselves, not others.

Children are copiers which can be a quick and efficient way to learn. Fathers provide role models that boys in particular are programmed to learn from, presumably for vital primal hunting purposes. In the absence of fathers, boys may follow celebrity examples which is not ideal as their understanding of celebrities is entirely superficial and provides inadequate foundations invariably accompanied by unsuitable goals.

The gender of parents teaches opposite sex children what to expect from, and how to respond to, the opposite sex in later life. This is applied in adult relationships, and feasibly more so if no opposite sex siblings have been present.

The Games

In my experience parenting is a daunting, if hugely gratifying, task. I admire anyone who takes it on and manages to do even a reasonable job, especially where several children are involved. It is an art more than a science, and possibly some of us are better endowed than others in it's nuances.

Parenting contains no shortage of stumbling blocks though, like – being controlling, smothering or judgemental. The infant must derive effective strategies to deal with whatever approaches it's carers employ, which tailors the child's behaviour and determines much of how they address the world in adulthood.

Some adults have children to secure the love they missed from their own parents. This is futile, and because the camouflaged goal of the parent is to take love *from* the child, the child remains at least partly 'unloved' and is likely to repeat the cycle with future generations unless they learn a lot in the meantime. Babies rely on parents. No matter how many hugs and kisses a parent extracts from a baby, it is probably just responding as instructed by it's powerful comforter and provider. If you observe carefully you will see it is normally the parent who is focusing the child on affection-giving behaviours for the sake of the parent, not the child. Touch and affection are important to children, the parent's reciprocal expectations are another matter.

The folly of seeking to gratify our childhood needs in adulthood through our children is another facet of the obsolete fear based ego concept. It's worth re-emphasising how this works (or fails to) – If we often felt something lacking in childhood, there is a strong possibility the need will become rooted in our psyche. It might then be automatically carried into adulthood and projected onto anything which reflects our past desires in some way. By failing to spot our old needs are no longer appropriate, harm can be done to ourselves and those we ought to cherish.

As we covered earlier, the attention we give to our children is a template for later life. When parents give too much, the child comes to expect this from the world and is eventually consistently disappointed or settles for dependent relationships with some sort of substitute 'supplier'. If the parents give too little, the child can grow to see the world and everyone in it as a means to obtain what they are 'owed'. Any such expectation or intention, learned in childhood from naive 'interpretations' of our parents' actions, contributes to adult frustration and unhappiness.

In more complex scenarios parents, inadvertently or otherwise, play emotional 'games' with their children which leave the child scared, confused and reluctant to criticise them. In these 'games', approval is switched on and off by parents or made clearly conditional. Also, conflicts between parents might lead to manipulation or generous attention as part of a strategic alliance with the child. In these circumstances the confused child may feel afraid, or very 'loved' indeed by periods of closer attentiveness. The consequent increase in emotional involvement leads to them dreading the ever-present threat of parental withdrawal or demands. Where parents have widely different views, or if their moods swing markedly, children are bound to be confused and similarly affected. The child fails to see that the parent is the problem more than the solution; even so, it is the only show in town. This sets him or her up for a future of tricky relationships where their *former* needs and fears are the real (albeit hidden) problem in adult life. Accordingly, acquiring what you think you need in this world may give temporary relief however it can lead to long-term frustration, fuelling further 'needs' and hence restlessness, when it is based on expired requirements, as is regularly the case.

The Pushing

'The road to hell is paved with good intentions.'

We all want what's best for our kids... or do we?

There is a regrettable common assumption at the centre of some parents' attitudes towards children. We mistakenly believe our children belong to us. Yes we are responsible for their upbringing but that doesn't mean we own them. Our job is to give children the best possible start in life and then back off, encouraging them to find their own way, irrespective of how uncomfortable the letting go might feel.

All parents choose a path for their children, teaching or allowing them to be taught as they see fit. Unfortunately, most of us don't adequately consider the highly personalised and often outdated basis of our values that we foist onto children. Raising clones of ourselves, compensating for our 'failures' or trying to fulfil our desires through our children, sentences them to a life of subjugation, avoidance or rebellion. From the clingy to the demanding, insecure parents can stifle the very essence of children. Celebrity casualties with pushy parents who used their children as surrogate achievers, sometimes testify to the potential ramifications of this blind exploitation taken to extremes.

One sad effect of judgemental parenting is that it's inclined to engender long-term 'emotional constipation', with related adverse health and relationship consequences, in those unlucky enough to be on the receiving end.

The Anger

Anger is closely connected to fear, consequently a degree of anger towards authority figures such as parents is understandable. This appears as hostility, withdrawal or more complex strategies. The anger might be bottled-up and saved for the rest of the world, not parents, because our minds can be so steeped in fear of the consequences of their disapproval that we seldom confront them.

Several well-intentioned parents retain a lifelong financial hold (subtle or otherwise) over their children which can add to repressed anger, as well as compound and prolong the dependency trap.

Anger *may* be vented at parents from time to time although it is often more vehemently directed elsewhere, even at ourselves (sometimes contributing to depression). None the wiser, our world continually produces many examples of people harbouring buried anger towards their parents, 'taking revenge' on others at any opportunity. A typical instance would be, if we only see the opposite sex as a means to our own ends we could be angry at our opposite sex parent.

Strong examples of individuals 'angry' at their parents can be observed at the front of Political, Social and Religious activism. Extreme cases can end up in prison or worse.

The Obstacles

Parental influence is so deeply ingrained that continuing to pursue approval and reassurance from our parents throughout life is commonplace. We show them what we have achieved and run to them when things go wrong. We may even tell them our stories when they are no longer alive. This doesn't necessarily mean we always like or even respect our parents. It mainly means we seek their approval because, as children, their assistance was crucial to our survival. As adults we continue to 'rely' on them; old habits die hard.

If you want to learn about someone, learn about their early relationship with their parents. If you want to understand yourself, learn about your early relationship with your parents. Numerous Psychologists will head straight to this and it is a wise approach. We appear to construct a script for life in childhood based on our parents as we see them (together with a few other factors) and carry this with us wherever we go. Yes they supplied some beneficial input but our parents came from a different age. They handed down *their* interpretations of the world based on *old* ideas. Politics, Religion, Nationalism, crime and judging the actions of others are common illustrations that can cause obstructions or diversions if we don't acknowledge their *past* basis.

One curious feature of modern society is how the useful knowledge that Psychologists alone have derived about parenting is rarely included in popular formative teaching. The requirement for cast-iron scientific proof is occasionally cited as good reason for this. A more plausible explanation for withholding such widely practical information is that everyone, including Psychologists, Leaders and Teachers must go through the parent pleasing process and it straightjackets the majority of us. Tight early parental reins remain in place preventing many from considering, let alone rectifying, faults.

Can you imagine trying to fix a machine while ignoring it's defective components. This is exactly what we do with humans and why our attempts to improve have become an elaborate game of snakes and ladders. We can't come up with best tactics to tackle life's impediments until we expose their root causes. That means admitting *we* are not perfect, and *our parents* were not perfect. There is no shame in that, nothing is perfect. Nevertheless, this admission of imperfection and it's causes can prove a major obstacle. Authority figures in particular often carry a heavier ego burden than most, which goes a long way to explaining why the challenge of acknowledging flaws defiantly remains i.e.

Large egos = higher levels of insecurity = appeal of power and control = less willingness to accept personal shortcomings.

In an ever-changing world, it helps to be aware of our conditioning. If we won't demystify our dominant drives and their sources, we are unlikely to adapt sufficiently to fresh situations. The constraints placed upon us by loyalty to obsolete programmed thinking leaves our lives less fruitful and overly awkward.

The Answer

Smoother progress could result from seeing the unsound basis of our reluctance to examine parental performance. As adults, we no longer have to rely on parental approval, or gain the approval of others as compensation. On the contrary, healthy natural development requires us to reduce our dependency on others and their influences. Neither is there any need to criticise parents. It's their effects we are interested in, not judging their intentions. Parents have their pluses as well as their minuses. Whatever they did was a result of *their* distinct backgrounds. Why should we continue to compound their unintentional 'errors'?

In any land, in any circumstances, we will live better if parents know how to do their most important job and do it well. This doesn't have to be left to slim chance as at present, it can be learned now.

Where parents provide a reasonably balanced upbringing, their children are less liable to have a multiplicity of needs or fears about the world in adulthood. They may or may not be super-achievers because they really don't have to be. When children are 'loved' unconditionally by their parents they typically turn out more assured with less to prove in later life, and move forward naturally without always chasing recognition. They may stand up against unfairness at times, even with force, but they will not see it as a continuous crusade against rife oppression.

Proper parenting is most significant in the earliest years of childhood, and it doesn't entail smothering affection, constant attention or continual approval. A helpful description is – when the child is convinced you are on it's side, no matter what. Occasional correcting provides helpful guidance the child expects whereas threatening to abandon them in any way, or giving them cause to doubt loyalty, will be detrimental.

The tremendous benefits of balanced parenting compared to the costs of failure speak for themselves. Poor parenting leads to widespread anger and dependency; better parenting is likely to create happier healthier lives, more cooperation and less fear. The tilt of these scales could be critical to our future. By placing this fundamental issue at the front of our agenda we should substantially reduce the unnecessary suffering and enormous wasted effort caused by sweeping it under the carpet. Our task is to appreciate the natural role of parents and how it can be best incorporated into a modern world. Honest, non-judgemental consideration of the full reasons why many of us may have been ill-prepared for this privilege will help to shed light on our misunderstandings, hopefully making them a thing of the past. It really is that basic.

Meanwhile, we still have a few *other* related obstructions compromising our vision...

Under The Influence

Humans absorb much more than we imagine. It's an efficient system, sometimes. What we take in often requires no thought, saving effort, although the downside of this is we are all too often unaware of our intake and it's effects. In some cases, like the air we breathe, the need to think about what we absorb will only be triggered by recognisable difficulties or changes. This probably saved us developing specific sensory mechanisms at the cost of other useful faculties but it can be one shortcut too many in the case of odourless toxic gases, for example. We have another related natural labour saving technique – our readiness to take the familiar for granted. Tendencies like these raise an interesting question – Just how much are our surroundings affecting us without our knowledge? Remember people worked with toxic paint, asbestos and radiation for years before their harm was detected. Smoking, alcohol and rich diets were seen as desirable until their damage became clear.

Some influences are helpful, some are not, and most of us don't recognise the extent and consequences of our regular exposure. If you are in any doubt about the subtlety or power of our influences let me give you a prime example in one word – ACCENTS. We rarely consider the everyday intake which automatically produces a range of highly distinctive accents. They illustrate how we miss obvious factors that impact on our lives immensely. The majority of us pick up accents without a moments thought and they can be life changing.

People are regularly put-off by accents. A big customer or potential employer could dislike our accent, which we simply absorbed. Likewise, *we* might not want to listen to others who speak in a certain way. Our distaste of some accents could prevent us from dealing with helpful or interesting people, even when we admit that the aversion comes from very personal associations. Nevertheless, if we find it irritating to listen to an accent, many of us will not persevere (our inability to decipher some accents doesn't help). This reaction seems extreme but it has a flip-side. We like some accents a lot, and employers have found that a few accents are generally better received by customers. This can be the determining factor when locating a business, clearly demonstrating how hidden input can alter our prosperity.

Superficial signals such as appearances, accents and language can arouse automatic stereotyping and cultural barriers. Similarly, we have all acquired a range of programmed presumptions that go unnoticed. Improved awareness of this might reduce our negative responses and resistance without necessarily making us like things we previously disliked. Wise avoidance may still be our best bet, rather than involvement with situations we find wearing. The main thing is, we will be less liable to compound any difficulties by blaming others for our reactions.

Short-Term Exposure

Background music is on the increase because it tampers with our mood. It acts as a catalyst for messages arriving in our brain. This is apparent when songs or pieces of music trigger strong memories from the distant past with related powerful emotions. Music can invigorate and depress us. From sport to nature, science to drama, nationalism to charitable causes, we are continually being 'told what to feel' by musical accompaniments. Recently I watched a painting on TV while two contrasting pieces of music were played in the background, one after the other. My emotional responses to the same picture were entirely different depending on the music. Try switching off the sound from a drama, documentary or sports match on television and see how the tension subsides. This raises valid concerns. Where else is it happening? How much are we really thinking and feeling for ourselves? What can we do about this and why bother anyway?

Music is only a trailer for the main event. The people we mix with, the work we do, our families, our entertainment, the places we visit, the newspapers we read, our surroundings, our interests, our beliefs and countless types of exposure we barely understand like food, water, weather and what is in the atmosphere all affect the human sponge.

For anyone who disputes our susceptibility, I would *suggest* watching a stage hypnotist at work. (I've never actually been present at such hilarity but I have watched snippets.) Granted, people are picked based on suitability and many are rejected. Still, the effects are staggering. 'I will snap my fingers and you will run around and cluck like a chicken,' says the hypnotist. He clicks his fingers and sure enough, the enthusiastic human 'hen' complies. Over and over, increasingly ridiculous behaviour is suggested and, to our amazement, the subjects obey without hesitation. Bizarre this may be and it is certainly selective for entertainment purposes, even so it is very telling about the power suggestion can have on us when our guard is down. Or what about cult members and fanatical followers of oppressive political regimes? Are we really that easily led, and is it happening right now without us ever knowing? The answer is surely an emphatic, YES!

You don't have to be a fashion victim to see how readily we copy others. As well as clothing, our near automatic inclination to replicate aspects of some group image can be seen in our home décor, our hairstyles, our gadgets, our topics of conversation and almost every other walk of life. As soon as anything becomes unfashionable we drop it like a hot potato. When most people are embracing something, we either join the throng or the opposition. Few perceive that the options and where we stand on them merely represent variations of routine approaches. True originality is rare due to saturating influences. If we managed to look beyond these, new inspiring possibilities might emerge.

Longer-Term Exposure

Our bodies digest weather information from their surroundings then change to suit the climate, but only after a while and up to a point. Skin colour, hair, eyes and respiratory systems are prime examples. (Some say the narrower eyes of far eastern people are a legacy from sustained brightness during an ice age 30,000 years ago.)

Light skin is more prone to damage in sunlight than dark skin. On the other hand, vitamin deficiencies, seemingly attributable to *insufficient* sunlight, can cause serious health problems. This indicates there may be risks living in climates that don't suit our inherited personal physiology.

On top of the physical effects of climate, it seems depression can also be due to a lack of sunlight; and the old saying, 'In spring a young man's fancy turns to women,' appears to have a chemical basis activated by increasing sunlight after winter. This points to possible additional connections between our *mental* state and the fittingness of our environment.

The integral process of adjusting to our surroundings is well demonstrated by all other life forms as they evolve to survive. Extinction is the price of failure to adapt. With this in mind, our attempts to provide controlled internal atmospheres could have severe side-effects. Apart from incubating bugs, they bypass certain adapting mechanisms which is liable to reduce these abilities in the longer-term, leading to less flexibility and greater dependency on technology. When we limit our exposure to environmental changes, we fail to allow sufficient exercise for our natural acclimatising, and end up paying the price in weakness and restriction.

We delight in breathtaking scenery and pay a premium for hotel rooms with sea views. Why? Because we like them. Yes, but why do we like them? That is the next logical question, and there are bound to be good reasons. Do we ever consider this or the effect our geographical location and outlook might be having on us? Are open views preferred as they enabled our ancestors to see threats and opportunities better? Do we feel liberated by expansive views? Is it the unobstructed light that arouses positive feelings? Is it a temporary high reaction to normally being cooped up? The sea contained food and exploration opportunities throughout most of our past, is that the appeal? Is the sound of the sea and water comforting because it reminds us of the womb? Are our sea origins a factor? We are mostly made of water and need plenty to survive, could that be significant?

Conversely, certain environments and restricted views can be very unappealing. Looking out on urban decay or ravaged landscapes is deflating. Small or obstructed windows usually frustrate us, but why? The truth is nobody really knows.

Our responses to vistas or climates could imply important connections. Science is attempting to unravel these mysteries. In the meantime, common sense suggests that enclosed conditions or totally alien environments might not be the ideal choices for us.

More appropriately…

From the outset humans had to come to terms with the fundamentals of their regions. Food could be subject to seasonal availability so our bodies and our nature will have learned this. Moving as required to find food and shelter would have been sensible survival tactics for us in the past. This means exploring! Without too much study, I think we could safely say that the not inconsiderable proportions of our legs support this, in more ways than one. (They're also a rather glaring and frequently overlooked design clue to our intended functioning, and the inappropriateness of spending too much time on our backsides indoors.) It follows then, that walking outdoors is likely to be an important part of a healthy human lifestyle. If further evidence is necessary, exploring and examination characteristics are major features of human childhood. Children often show us what comes naturally and it is a pity we miss their handy tips. At best we simply fail to understand, although usually we take the more blinkered approach of forcing them onto a frustrating set path which has little call for little explorers or *real* explorers of any kind.

A degree of contact with viruses supposedly helps to strengthen our immunity and improve our survival capabilities. Notably, in this regard, many Europeans shared accommodation with animals until recently which improved their resistance to animal based diseases. When Europeans moved into South America vast populations of natives died, partly because they had not lived as closely to animals and therefore were overcome by viruses that the foreigners carried obliviously.

In addition to hard won immunities, humans formed various mutually profitable associations with animals over thousands of years. Like any capabilities, these fade if they're not fostered. In towns and cities animal numbers are inevitably relatively low, leading to disconnection and eventual avoidance of most animals. This can become apprehension turning to fear. Our answer has been to tame some as pets or study them in the confinement of zoos, providing limited interaction and benefits. There is much more we can learn from *wild* animals about our natural selves and the outside world.

Lately, animal 'predators' have been re-introduced to communities (re-wilding) in an attempt to restore balance. This is not straightforward as it contains risks and dangers for us as well as advantages. Many of the dangers arise from our shortage of involvement with animals and consequent diminished coping skills. The interesting part is, we now appear to be learning more about natural equilibrium and life's required trade-offs.

Partial Perspective

They say there is no such thing as reality, merely perspective i.e. we see the world as *we* are, not as it is. For instance,

Police and legal workers might be inclined to have a crime emphasised view of the world. Emergency doctors deal with dramas daily which could colour their attitudes. The Military may have rigid views of authority or feel multiple threats exist. These are the obvious distorting implications of our narrow work model. Beyond lies a wider issue – although some of us are overexposed to specific areas of life, many are underexposed to key realities. This imbalance has two striking drawbacks. Firstly we fail to experience an adequate picture of the world, and secondly we fail to acquire sufficient expertise to cope with it effectively.

In our personal lives, doing the same type of things with the same kind of people in the same sort of places exacerbates insular mindsets. We eagerly gravitate towards what feels comfortable and avoid what doesn't, failing to obtain ample fresh exposure. Essentially, we reinforce set norms constantly and are subtly re-affected by them without detection. People who repeatedly pick abusive partners because of childhood conditioning illustrate our 'familiarity at any cost' technique. Familiarity may be predictable but we have lost our way forward and this creates stagnation in our lives. Stagnation is a lack of flow which causes discontent and ill health in humans just as it makes water smell foul. The bulk of our activities and travels represent little more than running faster in bigger circles that supply variations on the same themes.

Conceivably, modern human failure to flow, mix, explore and really change is caused by an early childhood need for security persisting undetected. This insecurity breeds repetitive patterns of behaviour as we pursue predictability or control due to our previous interpretations of not being in control. By failing to recognise our predicament and it's sources, life turns into a treadmill eased by distractions at best. We may even feel peculiarly reassured periodically despite being devoid of fulfilment.

Soldiering On

Frustration, agitation and disillusionment are among the short-term products of our closed loop lifestyles. In the medium-term we reduce our ability to adapt as we use it less. Longer-term we are in big trouble if we stifle our exploring faculties and settle for versions of what is familiar.

Our lives are affected by an array of factors we mostly remain oblivious to. Sometimes we stray too far from what is healthy and in other ways we don't explore enough. The surprising thing is not that this lack of awareness and it's consequences makes us upset, confused or ill; the surprise is how we have managed to get by this way so far. Our resilience is indisputably impressive but how much can it handle?

Moods

Some days I jump out of bed full of the joys, other days I venture up grudgingly. I take a liking to a type of food or music for weeks, even months, and then go off it entirely. These are what I call moods. We sometimes call them phases or impulses depending on their duration. When our mood changes we see things differently, demonstrating how much the world reflects back the way *we* are.

A girl *once told me to remember this always – 'When a woman says she doesn't want to see you ever again, she means for a week, maybe two at the most.' My adviser was adamant, and still I forgot on important occasions when it would have been beneficial but I'm learning, slowly.*

Changing moods don't just apply to women and relationships, they affect most of our lives. We make many regrettable choices based on our moods. The wise advice to, 'Never go shopping (for food) hungry,' warns against the impulsive power of our appetites. We join something enthusiastically, participate a few times, then lose interest. The truth is, our better reasoning is all too often overruled by moods and emotions, so we can slip up big style when we fail to take them into account.

Moods may be enveloping but they pass, possibly sooner than we expect. They can be caused by our thoughts, the weather, what someone said, what we saw or thought we saw, a smell, a song, a memory, a loss, a gain or any multitude of things. Our moods, like our personality, are unique to us and if we want to make better choices we should pay more (or less) attention to our moods.

Reacting

In our world of lost people, reactions and responses have a lot to answer for.

Isaac Newton showed that – 'To every action there is an equal and opposite reaction.' His five suspended silver balls (Newton's Cradle) provide a convincing demonstration of this. That's fine for silver balls, even for animals reacting is pretty much the best they can do, and we could excuse children. However, is it not somewhat irresponsible for adult humans to let this go unchecked so regularly?

Our instinctive responses have their place. They reduce wasted effort in routine tasks and can be life saving in some instances. Racing drivers place great emphasis on their instinctive reactions. That said, few of us are going to be racing drivers any time soon, so it seems the best places for spontaneous reactions are when we have either no time or no need to think.

Everyday thoughtless reacting creates all kinds of turmoil. In the heat of the moment we can say and do the awfullest things. Our emotions are in overdrive and our perspective is temporarily skewed. Sometimes we are effective, usually we are not. The situation grows ever more complex when insecurity (often experienced as anger) makes us defend our emotional gaffes remorselessly. Then the work required to mend the disruption is increased out of all proportion. Time after time this happens and still we continue to suffer at our own hands.

We remain at the mercy of our reactions because they were programmed into us long ago. Having observed and applied them so many times they became automatic, and we acquired powerful impulses to obey their commands.

With a clearer head after the dust has settled, we ought to realise everyone including ourselves is prone to overreacting at times. This admission is not a weakness, it takes real strength. Acceptance of our less constructive tendencies helps to mend fences and improve outcomes in future. Mistakes are valuable learning opportunities for the wise –

'Wise men make mistakes, fools repeat them.'

Extra Snags

A careless word or action can have serious repercussions but these rarely compare to the preset life choices we make. Our friends, partners, work and environment are often determined by embedded responses. This 'handy' mental shortcut of applying what things and people *represent* to us, is frequently misleading. For instance, most of us don't know much about Seals. They may be a menace to fish stocks or necessary prey for other creatures, still we don't like them being harmed because they look cute. Similarly Polar Bears seem cuddly and appealing (from a safe distance), despite being savage predators. Repeatedly we make choices based on emotions that are sparked by surface impressions rather than requisite data.

Won't the instructions we received as children help? 'Don't do this. Don't do that. Always remember to, etc.'

Unfortunately, mere instructions can cause more harm than good in adult life if we don't understand the basis of our reactions. Overlaid rules and regulation, combined with a lack of informed thinking, conspire to deliver escalating problems and failures.

When we are driven to act and react habitually, we are unlikely to be utilising our range of faculties to their best advantage. A step back, seeing persistent tendencies and their consequences, considering another view or taking more time can help enormously.

Relationships

A traveller arrived at the gates of a city. Before entering he asked the gatekeeper what the people inside were like. The gatekeeper asked what the people were like in the city the traveller had come from. 'They were a selfish, disagreeable lot mostly,' replied the traveller. 'Well, I expect you will find them much the same here,' said the gatekeeper.

Later another traveller arrived making the same enquiry, and the gatekeeper asked his question again. 'Well,' replied the latest traveller, 'The people in my last city were friendly and kind on the whole.' 'I expect you will find them much the same here,' said the gatekeeper.

We conjure up expansive ideas about others and their personalities from minimal information. It could be their tone of voice, size, shape or jacket that triggers our attraction, indifference or disapproval. Perhaps we haven't seen the person or spoken to them but we already have an idea if we like them or not. This styles our attitudes and colours any involvement, often confirming the picture we previously constructed, or 'the box we put them in' from what we had available. It's reassuring to find we were correct all along – 'If only everyone *knew* people the way we do.'

It helps to split relationships into three main categories for explanation purposes – Partners, Friends and Colleagues. Let's head for the juiciest one first.

Partners

As a species our survival to date has depended not only on reproduction involving a man and a woman, but also their bonding. Nature apparently provides indicators which draw us to those who seem compatible and help us avoid others who don't, normally without us noticing what is at work. On top of this we accumulate layers of partly undetected persevering preferences, making new versions of previous encounters virtually inevitable.

The sources of attraction in non-reproductive partnering such as same sex, companionship and 'caring' relationships include variations on the standard themes that can be illuminating. I will leave their exploration to anyone with a specific interest.

Whatever is occurring, examining our own drives can yield a few surprises and provide helpful alerts in the coupling minefield.

I was at a party with my partner at the time, where we met a good friend I have known for many years. When he saw her he exclaimed, 'They all look the same!' I questioned this and he re-emphasised, 'They all...look...THE SAME!' I've had very few close partners; they varied in appearance and seemed quite different people to me. So I let it go and put the remark down to his fondness for a tipple. Years later I realised he was spot on (outsiders see things we are too close to notice). Not long after learning about the lasting power of early experiences, I soon tied in every partner with my favourite childhood companion – my grandmother. This may not come across as the most flattering comparison to women but it certainly is in my book. Although feasibly they displayed facets of her temperament, my gran's familiar longish dark hair was probably the main pull, and it still is (in spite of a few tough lessons that cast serious doubt over it's reliability).

Certain characteristics and appearances have a broad appeal whereas some might please one individual more than another. We are consistently drawn to those who feel comfortable or familiar and allow us to play the limited parts we learned in childhood or early adulthood. People who offer what we appear to lack also attract us and we try to avoid anyone who represents what we have learned to dislike about ourselves or others. If we like our parents or siblings, we may pick similar partners. If not, we may avoid anyone who resembles them. If we like aspects of our appearance we will be attracted to them in others or vice-versa. If we think we are overweight we may be attracted to slim people. If status is important to us we may be attracted to power or wealth. If we feel weak we may be attracted to others who appear strong. If lack of intelligence in ourselves or close family was an issue in childhood, we might be attracted to 'clever' people. The childhood 'victim' can be attracted to others who confirm their victim status and resulting view of the world. The outwardly strong but secretly insecure person could be attracted to someone they can control to an extent, and on it goes.

Consequently, if we feel smug when others find us appealing or snubbed when they don't, it would be worth bearing in mind that they are usually affected by what we *represent* to them, at least as much as anything else.

Given the choice of female physical features, surveys suggest that men are most attracted to the 'waist to hips' ratio of women, which is intuitively taken as a key factor in child bearing. By far the single most significant physical factor in women's attraction to men turned out to be height. This is a primal pointer towards the man being an effective protector and provider. (As an extension of this – other data indicates women are twice as likely as men to dream of having sex with celebrities.) These are generalisations of course and unique combinations that incorporate appearance, personality and status preferences will be involved in each case.

We like to be liked, which can be one of the most compelling components in attraction for approval seekers –

> *A mother asked her son what his new girlfriend liked about him. 'She thinks I'm good looking, intelligent, funny and a great dancer,' he confidently replied. 'And what do you like about her?' his mother continued. 'Well, she thinks I'm good looking, intelligent, funny and a great dancer,' he repeated.*

Attraction is governed by a range of factors we have still to fully fathom. Smells are important to us and some people have a potent 'chemistry' (however so called 'chemistry' is often used as an excuse for impulsive involvement). Do we radiate 'energies', chemicals or electrical charges yet to be understood, along the lines of other species who attract or repel from afar? We hear about mysterious 'powers of attraction', and I can sometimes sense more than discomfort around particular people so maybe we *do* have avoidance radar too.

Duration

The length and stages of couples' attachment might not always be as arbitrary as we assume.

Apparently Nature has embedded timescales that affect relationship commencement, bonding and duration (although recent accelerated behaviour may blur the lines). It makes sense to consider these rather than automatically blaming ourselves or others for not conforming to conventional norms.

Men are instinctively interested in their own genes. For this reason they may be intuitively inclined to avoid 'commitment' to a woman for around four months, as a safeguard against the presence of other men's fertilising genes in her. (Perhaps they are unwittingly waiting for the bump to show, or not.) Women have their own priorities. It looks like they may be programmed to give a man a certain time to 'commit' and fertilise their eggs. A woman is apt to give-up around month 8, if at least part of this isn't happening. Her internal clock is ticking even if she doesn't realise it, or want children.

Broadly speaking, it looks like bonded human relationships are designed to last long enough for a single child to obtain a degree of independence at around 3 years of age. This suggests the natural cycle for human mating relationships is 4 years or thereabouts, after which both parents can 'move on' to increase the genetic diversity of their offspring. (Historically this could have improved average survival chances.) Modern divorce and separation rates reflect these timescales and it is proving troublesome for our societies to deal with their fallout in a world of greater choice and stimulation. This leaves us with a dilemma…

Respect for our instincts makes sense, always allowing them to control us is folly. An important feature of the human species is our capacity to question and refine our programming.

Close personal relationships involve a deep bonding aspect which our societies try to build on, rather than dismantle and replace every few years. Just because we were programmed by previous circumstances to regularly seek new partners, doesn't mean it is the most effective approach these days. Stepping back onto the relationship merry-go-round may look attractive to the uninitiated however, it can be highly disruptive and involve many unforeseen hitches. 'Out of the frying pan, into the fire,' so to speak.

Complications

Without modern societies our primal relationships were presumably more group based. Many women died in childbirth necessitating fallback carers for their children. Other women, especially grandmothers where available, could step in. Women ran the additional risk of being abandoned with children if other women attracted their men. This had serious implications as men were the principal providers and protectors. Hence one of the greatest threats to women has always been – other women! This combination of potential catastrophes created a curious paradox for women of dependency on 'rivals'. They probably used gossip and mixing closely with other women to monitor goings-on and improve the survival chances of their family. Also, men could be killed hunting so we could reasonably expect women to seek back-up males for this eventuality. The appeal of women to other men (flirting) likely contributed a welcome element of insurance in this event. Correspondingly, men could improve *their* chances of genetic success by fertilising various women, relying on them feeling naturally disposed to looking after any offspring where possible as they contained the mother's genes. Times have changed, nonetheless several of these bygone issues impact on our modern relationship dynamics. If you have any acquaintance at all with adult sexual relationships, it is highly likely you will be familiar with some of the many 'games' that can emerge.

In older cultures, extended families and tribes doubtless offered direction and support to reduce survival threats and guard against disharmony caused by any proliferation of our genetic insurance strategies. Their legacy can still be seen where old habits prevail. Nowadays we supply social and health care that reduces the need for individual family units to rely entirely on relatives. This allows us to loosen ties, mix, spread and move forward.

Friends

Friendships offer considerable flexibility, enhancing their value, and there has never been a time when 'meeting' and vetting new friends was easier. Unlike partners or colleagues, we can adjust our exposure as required, almost. As our circumstances change we can gain new friends.

We share interests with friends, socialise, and give mutual support or advice. Some friends come and go, some become life long companions out-lasting all other relationships. There are many types of friends – close friends, acquaintances, niche friends, opposite sex friends, old friends. All have one thing in common – us! We choose them and we routinely apply similar selection criteria.

What determines our choice of friends? Funnily enough, conditioning chiefly. We are unlikely to make friends with people we find disagreeable or irritating unless we have another agenda (in this case, the term 'friend' would be a misnomer). The bases of friendships don't merit extensive study here. Suffice to say, the friends we 'select' provide insight to the type of people we are and our requirements of others, as do most relationships.

Whatever our friendship inclinations, failure to explore them is a lost opportunity.

Colleagues

Successful managers will tell you work can be less about ability and more about compatibility. In many organisations, 'fitting-in' and not rocking the boat take priority over ability. Not all tasks centre on teamwork though. Effective leadership or creativity may require a radical approach from more individualistic characters. These good team players and creative leaders could be described as either end of the personality spectrum, whereas some jobs require a blend. So, to assist with the complexities of selection, psychological profiling is often used. This is a helpful tool when combined with other methods, but less so if relied upon entirely because the accuracy of the job specification and completeness of the psychological profile cannot be guaranteed.

Irrespective of the tests we apply, humans naturally head for what appeals to them and try to avoid what doesn't. We attempt to make any logic fit our feelings wherever possible. This is no less true in employee/job selection, and whether we recognise it or not our mind can be made-up about a candidate or a job within seconds during the first face to face meeting, or earlier. Yet again we prefer candidates and colleagues who look, act or sound like what appeals to us, or who possess some experience, qualification or attribute we admire. We discard those we find threatening or who display characteristics we dislike in ourselves or in general.

Pack instincts and pecking orders emerge at work, just as they do in families or social circles. Behaviour is tailored, intentionally or not, to suit. As the groups we participate in vary so do our techniques, in order to move towards what feels most comfortable or least uncomfortable.

Accordingly, our work and colleagues typically provide mere variations on standard interactions.

Sex

I've heard advice to have dogs spayed or neutered as soon as possible unless there is good reason not to. Seemingly it has a calming effect that stops them constantly thinking, 'I have to mate, I have to mate.' I don't claim to know what dogs think but I'm pretty sure humans spend a lot of time thinking about mating or we wouldn't have got this far. Sex is definitely natural although this time Nature, unchecked, leads us all over the place and right up the creek without a paddle.

The Drive Of Our Life

Natural drives exist for a reason. Rewards are attached to activities which sustain us, by our bodies producing chemicals that create enjoyable feelings – pleasure. You could say Nature makes eating enjoyable because we need food to live, and sex is made enjoyable because the continuation of our species relied upon it. Sex produces heightened pleasure, making it one of our most commanding impulses. Like most pleasures, it comes at a cost. Make no mistake, sex is not a recreation sport despite this popular mis*conception*.

Sex has a compelling message, easily conveyed and frequently used to lure us. Like children, we readily respond to simple seductive messages with power, such as The Child Catcher uses in the film Chitty Chitty Bang Bang. 'Lollipops, lollipops, come and get them children!' he cries. Ignoring every warning, the children run into his wagon containing the goodies to find they are trapped in a, not very well disguised, cage. The question is – if they knew it was a cage in the first place would they still have been lured? What would it take for them to see anything other than the treats?

We see what we *want* to see, and sex supplies a sharp focus to our childlike selective vision. Nature has given sex huge power so when we let this genie out of the bottle to play, a force that can cause havoc is unleashed. Don't get me wrong, I'm not condemning sex, it's wonderful. I'm explaining the intent and cost of it's allure. What we choose to do about it, if anything, is another matter.

Reliable contraception only appeared around the 1960's, which is very recent in terms of our species. Since then the cost of sex looks to have reduced considerably, especially for women. Pregnancy can be controlled without sacrificing pleasure, and both sexes feel they have discovered a new liberation. There is more to this story though, and there is more to sex. Nature has it's own ideas about sexual freedom. Historically, vast populations were wiped out by sexual infections, particularly when promiscuity took hold. Lately, devastating new sexual diseases have evolved, urging caution in relation to our indulgences. Constantly seeking sexual pleasure creates all kinds of complications and doesn't appear to make us any happier overall. What are we missing then?

Teamwork

For as long as we can tell, sex has had two essential functions (well, one function with two parts really). Firstly, and most evidently, to bring the seed and fertilising sperm together. Secondly, and almost as importantly, to form a bond between parents for the benefit of their children and gene survival. In Nature's formula, we can be fairly confident pleasure has been the means to attain these ends rather than an end in itself.

It appears men and women in 'committed' relationships have separate underlying priorities when it comes to sex, with the same ultimate common denominator – their own gene continuation (and possible enhancement). So how does Nature combine the interests of both parties effectively?

Part of the answer seems to be that the happiness of both sexes has become conditional on complementary nurturing factors. More obviously, most women feel especially good when they see their children happy. Less obviously, men are rewarded by seeing their children's mother happy, as this should mean she is more likely to nurture their offspring. When a man is 'in love' with a women he often enquires about her happiness and this is probably a prime innate motivator of his interest. When a woman enquires about the happiness of her male partner, it may relate to concern for the adequate provision and protection of her children, even if they don't exist.

Standards & Stability

Human reproductive coupling appears to be a cooperative male adaptation which provides an improved basis for progress, replacing the oppressive primal practice of alpha-male domination. Polygamous relationships, adopted by some cultures, may be a 'halfway house' system.

Recent changed circumstances cloud human partnering issues, hence a trip back in our convenient time-machine should help here.

In the past, women had to be very careful sexually. Apart from the diseases that threatened both sexes, women could not afford to get pregnant and abandoned by a man, as they would be literally 'left holding the baby' with little or no support. Remember, men were the protectors and providers. Looking after other men's genes is not the best tactic for males in the gene survival game, so women already pregnant or with children from another man could be far less attractive as partners. This natural preference for males to avoid investing in other men's genes goes a long way towards explaining why many men still prefer not to form their families around 'flirtatious' women. The male preference for 'reliable' women legacy also suggests that women inclined to caution (not abstinence) in sexual behaviour, might continue to be advantaged in their quest to attract and retain the 'best' males. They may also feel better about themselves, knowing sub-consciously they are providing their genes with favourable circumstances for paternal providing/protecting loyalty (necessary or not), rather than succumbing to risky short-term indulgences. (So think carefully before swallowing the seductive notion that women can readily act like opportunistic men and become happier. Women and men are suited to different roles, forged over many millennia not a mere half-century, which affect us differently at times for long-standing, deep-rooted reasons.)

Women, their families, their tribes and their religions doubtless publicly frowned on male gigolos because 'damaging a woman's reputation' could make her a burden, by reducing her chances of attracting adequate male support. (To what degree, privately as individuals, these groups practised what they preached is open to question.) It seems feasible that moral teachings from ancient religions and cultures were greatly influenced by this priority, as well as their experience of sexual disease risks. The women and cultures who learned how best to obtain men's family loyalty, to an extent at least, probably provided the genes for modern humans; possibly making us more suited to and rewarded by mutual loyalty, although this is a rather tenuous connection.

Ultimately, cooperative survival success would depend on our ability to keep philandering under control (or under wraps). So Nature and societies both seem to have learned this lesson and created their own tempering tools in tandem, with Nature apparently leading the way. Let's separate them...

Nature's Way – The possible natural mutual vetting timescales mentioned earlier, might play an important part in the genetically crucial commitment game. Men may take a few months to establish or observe if a woman is carrying another man's genes; women take time to weed out gigolos and other undesirables (courting, vetting and referral are such devices). Like many infections, sexually transmitted diseases proliferate with mixing, urging caution and limitations. Intriguingly this care improves trust and cooperation, together with our survival prospects. However, taken to extremes, overly restricted sexual exposure leading to 'in-breeding' creates dysfunctions which *reduce* survival chances.

Society Safeguards – The fundamental importance and complexities of relationships, cooperation and reproduction have led societies to adopt a multitude of well-intentioned precautions aimed at ensuring the power of our sex drives is handled responsibly. These help in some ways and hinder in others. Arranged marriages reduce a few risks, while creating their own drawbacks. Many religions, based on historical cultures, heavily repress sexuality using simplified, underdeveloped moral judgements that now require improved explanation. Marriage ceremonies, originally designed to foster commitment, have become devalued as intimate vows are made and increasingly discarded. (That said, total commitment can be calamitous in dire circumstances). Practical measures such as child-benefit payments may encourage adults to fulfil their financial obligations but they cannot begin to make-up for the distress caused to children by broken families.

Again, clearer understanding *coupled* with a balanced approach appears to be our best way forward.

Beyond The Lollipops

The full power of Nature lies behind the purpose and responsibilities of sex. Consequently, where we fail to comply, and see it as some sort of all-night candy store, we get sick. This can show up in an incessant pursuit of gratification, a lack of satisfaction, reduced self-esteem or broken homes, lives and societies. I'm not moralising here, that's less than useless. What I'm suggesting is that if we learn how to appreciate what underlies our strongest drives, we can perhaps benefit from them and reduce unnecessary difficulties. Happy families and committed partners, who escape the lure of brief sexual thrills, do exist. Probably they were dealt a hand that predisposed them to being more content or careful. They may not make sensational media fodder but their stories form the basis of many feel-good themes that can warm our hearts. Yes, there is a childhood 'desire for love' aspect in our positive responses to these romantic tales although there is evidently much more.

The rewards of sex have always come with limitations and responsibilities which birth control fails to eradicate. Understandably a promiscuity surge flowed from the sudden elimination of certain sexual consequences, in this latest false dawn for risk free indulgence – remember Isaac Newton's colliding silver balls, 'To every action there is an equal and opposite reaction.' These promiscuity swings may be a natural response to suddenly changed circumstances, but pleasure and pain are said to be two sides of the same coin in Nature's action/reaction balancing act.

For those who haven't yet reached the conclusion that care and moderation is the best policy, all I can say is examine the evidence. Closer scrutiny of indulgent lifestyles, now and throughout history, reveals casualty after casualty continually chasing thrills to avoid the pain or emptiness caused by their hollow lives and state of mind. Conversely, lasting happiness has a lot to do with understanding and accepting ourselves and our responsibilities. If we act like children, constantly sneaking treats which have been carefully rationed for good reasons, we will be dragged around by our untamed appetites time after time while we miss out elsewhere.

The Language Of Lust

If I haven't spouted sufficient cold water to totally dampen all ardour, and anyone retains enough hot blood pumping through their veins to appreciate one of life's greatest gifts, here are a few insights that should prove helpful –

Passionate kissing is probably based on the intimate bonding and nurturing effect of mothers traditionally chewing food for babies and passing it from mouth to mouth.

Breasts apparently have a prime sexual attraction function beyond feeding babies – no surprise there then. They likely represent buttocks, and tie in with lips which mirror the flushing sexual signals of female genitalia that have now become concealed by our upright posture (as opposed to other primates). These provide strong sexual signals in our most noticeable areas. (Bright red lipstick will never look the same again.)

Certain body language like dilated pupils. mirroring posture or gestures, and feet pointing towards someone indicates attraction or interest.

Mutual grooming and sharing food contribute to adult bonding, as they do between parents and children.

Women are inclined to show more flesh when ovulating.

Women's tendency to favour lying down after sex is conceivably inked to aiding their fertilisation process. Men have no such requirement.

I will leave you to enjoy discovering more for yourself, responsibly I hope.

Gender

Men are male, women are female. Nothing too taxing there. Having said that, the sources and implications of this bedrock detail are regularly overlooked. In fact, there is science that implies gender differences may not be as significant as they appear. Nonetheless, for our purposes, it helps to consider a few recurring dissimilarities. One of my consistent threads is Nature's design, and the design of men and women differs for pertinent reasons. Obviously I am generalising here of course, and now having offered that handy disclaimer it's into the fire...

Again we have to bear in mind that everything in Nature is built for a purpose or purposes, and failure to function as intended makes life tricky. Over countless years, men have been configured to fertilise women's eggs, hunt, explore, protect and provide. Correspondingly, women previously needed to attract men and retain them for a while to maximise the chances of themselves and their offspring surviving. Although there are many other tasks, our physiology and behaviour clearly point to these factors being central.

Male attitudes veer towards logic and practicality, no doubt because providing and protecting were strategic, dangerous and vital for everyone. Women are disposed towards emotions and perhaps intuition, presumably because babies don't deal in dialogue. Men readily offer unwanted practical solutions to women merely venting their feelings, and both parties typically fail to grasp the mix-up. (Women are more apt to express and share emotions whereas men were accustomed to *confronting* threats and *seizing* opportunities, or at least assessing their scale, rather than just providing sounding-boards.) These variations account for some of the reasons why men and women can be bamboozled by one another.

Boys Will Be Boys

Seemingly some data indicates that the only school subjects where boys consistently outperform girls involve spacial skills. That means anything to do with distances, shapes and directions. This, combined with other traits and pent-up energy, points to the inappropriateness of routinely confining boys and men. (The tendencies of boys also suggest they benefit from a degree of competition, teamwork, adventure and positive male role models.) Could it be that we are not making the most of their skills by sitting boys in classrooms or in front of screens from an early age? Given the right circumstances and opportunity most children want to explore, and boys are predominantly cut out for this. I come from a Work Study background and my experience is that women are more able to do routine work in confined environments than men. Women can 'switch-off' more easily, which could tie in with child adaptation capabilities. Switching-off a little may be useful in the care of demanding children whereas it would be extremely hazardous while hunting or exploring, leading to disastrous consequences for an entire family or tribe.

Tackling threats has always been a prime function of men. To date, wars have been fought and critical conflicts settled by men in the vast majority of cases. Although fighting is far from ideal in a civilised world, males of many large animal species can be seen throughout Nature settling disputes using versions of this last resort. Posturing, compromise and withdrawal are well-tested tools in damage limitation that can prevent escalation. Due to their other priorities, women lack this primal experience. Hence, female fracas may be more emotional (especially when their opponent is of the same sex – remember one of the biggest threats to women used to be other women). This doesn't mean females cannot do otherwise. Nor does it mean men are superior to women, oh no, both parties bring attributes to the table in various forms.

As far as I can work out, historically men have been the gender tasked with moving forward, making them more inclined to take risks on average. Women contribute beneficial balance in the progress partnership by tending towards consolidation. They also demonstrate important contingency qualities i.e. – when men fail to deliver sufficient progress, women will often badger them and eventually take on the role (in part, at least) if possible. Though useful, this fallback option is rarely ideal.

Men don't seem to multi-task as well as women and this points to a male emphasis on focus, veering towards obsession. Roles like childcare call for a range of simultaneous attentive skills; hunting, exploring and protecting on the other hand can require concentration on specifics for lengthy periods. Men seem to be at the extremes of most things, from mass murder to art and science, indicating a significant degree of intensity in aspects of their make-up.

I am not suggesting this is the full story by any means. My point is that we are again missing the point, to our cost.

From their earliest ages, boys are being groomed for roles which mostly don't use fundamental aptitudes. Society doesn't know what to do about this yet, choosing to ignore it while forcing males to swim against their tide or languish in the shallows. The positive male contribution has become stifled in much of modern society, creating a failure to provide the natural balance that healthy advancement requires. (Oppressive male domination, which can still be seen in certain cultures, is the opposite extreme.) Inevitably some boys and men will find problematic outlets for their aptitudes and energy, in a typical 'devil makes work for idle hands' compensation attempt to deal with the situations we have created. Lots get frustrated, angry, depressed or desperate.

What Women Want…

…is likely to be heavily influenced by thousands of years of dependency on men, that has only changed recently. Recent changes don't count for much where natural drives are concerned so it helps to revisit our formative history again. The recurring challenge for women has been to satisfy their nurturing instincts while pursuing whatever else seems necessary or appealing.

Apparently surveys indicate that girls outperform boys generally in every school subject apart from Physics and Spacial Skills. This doesn't necessarily mean girls are brighter than boys in most subjects. It could be that boys are disadvantaged by circumstances. Nevertheless, plainly girls are relatively bright overall. Therefore, the subservient past role of women could have been a frustrating 'needs must' situation, accounting for the eagerness of some to 'compensate'. That aside, women will have developed to make the most of their position with a little help from mother nature. Games have always been played between genders to have their 'needs' met, as we all know.

From observing ancient tribes, women look like the busier gender. In fact, keeping busy appears to be a key part of their happiness. Visits to old tribes suggest their women are content living this way, no matter how unlikely it sounds to us. To get a better picture of why this could be we need a wider view of what shaped women over time. Until lately, many women died in childbirth. Without modern contraception, those who survived spent a lot of time pregnant, had several children to look after and high infant mortality to deal with. While men were hunting and exploring (which women also did to a lesser extent), women would be attending to the numerous immediate everyday family tasks. In short, most women were pretty busy, and accustomed to it.

These days many women are entangled in a mesh of misunderstandings...

Originally our society was designed and dominated by men, some say it still is. Whoever is in control (if anyone) is questionable, all we know is – times have changed. Work in society no longer suits most men – indoor, mental more than physical, repetitive, heavily structured. Women now play a much bigger part in 'work' although they have inherited the male legacy of what work requires. Consequently, a number of women seem to be trying to act like men when it comes to work. Such women *can* be successful in the world of work, if you subscribe to a selective view of success; whereas a bit of behind the scenes information would perhaps shed light on the ramifications elsewhere in their lives.

As we grow wealthier and automation replaces physical work, many more women have time, energy and money to spare, even if they don't care to admit it. Like men, their energy has to go somewhere and all too often it turns into drama and self-obsession. Predictably, obsessiveness in women has a lot to do with appearances, due to conditioning derived from their primal motivation to attract men – 'Does my bum look big in this?' Lotions, potions, makeovers, hairstyles, shopping, eating, dieting and a multitude of other distractions are all manifestations of an imbalance which has hit both women and men. (Some women don't just rely on the appearances game for attention. Other attraction devices include status, wiles, generosity and support.) They may not be interested in having children or more children, and they may be perfectly capable of providing for themselves financially; all the same, many women strive as never before to be 'attractive' in comparison to 'the competition'. This preoccupation is a distortion caused in great part by Nature's traditional compensating activities being reduced or eliminated. The resulting void leads to anxiety and insecure self-centredness. These in turn drive our consumer society, but where to?

Challenge

Most of us yearn for the easy life. When we get a break we wish it could last forever. 'Easy' lifestyles are selectively portrayed by the media and advertisers to attract us, and we fall for it because we are drawn to what appears to be missing from our own lives. Strangely though, we grow restless and bored after a while without enough to do. This apparent contradiction is a good example of how little we can trust our brains to predict the lasting appeal of what appears attractive now.

When you boil it down, life is a challenge. It always has been and probably needs to be. Some challenges are fun, some are interesting and a few can feel unbearable. In any event, we often hear that challenges contain our most valuable lessons, and I can testify to that. Humans are the products of challenges and we respond to them in our own ways. We won't always prevail but we need suitable challenges for adequate living, whatever the outcomes.

Natural enthusiasm for challenges is clearly evident in our children. Yes, they lack good judgement and a grasp of dangers but that won't stop them trying. After a setback they will be up and at it again in the light of their latest experience, unless they are considerably damaged or prevented. By cosseting our children we inhibit their natural appetite for challenges, hindering development and creativity. Subjected to restricting concerns they become stifled. (Children's activities are increasingly monitored and we have yet to see the full consequences of this close control on coming generations.)

Like inhibited children, we have suppressed our spirit for exploration and stimulating challenge, as our pendulum has swung towards more comfort, contrived exploits and fear of failure. Challenges are developmental exercises. They encourage resourcefulness and provide outlets for our physical and mental abilities. Like a plant or wild animal, we have to make the best of our situation. That is what shapes and rewards us. Without the right challenges we get obsessive, complacent and 'sick', unwilling then unable to face life on *it's* terms. Avoiding new challenges and not taking appropriate risks is very risky, in the longer term.

If you want to recline forever in the lap of luxury, think again. It isn't healthy! Some of the biggest smiles are seen on the faces of people who deal with difficult circumstances every day. That doesn't mean their conditions are ideal by any means. Perhaps their lesson is – *ideal* is not the answer… if it even exists?

Ability

Humans possess a range of different capabilities and complementary skills that have brought us to where we are now, and natural selection is a ruthless arbiter that removed many of our less effective predecessors. Luck certainly played a part, but to be here our genes must have overcome a multitude of recurring obstacles over aeons. Surely this requires extraordinary attributes combined with powerful resilience. Despite everyone achieving this remarkable feat, many of us think we are obviously 'superior' to those around us. We *are* different for sure, but better?... I doubt it. Once more, our partisan egos are busily at work creating divisive delusions. This causes us all to suffer, so let's see if we can expose that obstinate fraudster again by taking in a few other angles.

Like children, we habitually judge people based on appearances at first. Qualifications, status, clothes, cars, houses, all style our views. We were taught to think like this in our earliest years by a blinkered world that appreciates only a very limited number of attributes. At school or pre-school we also learned about our own abilities, or did we? I think we more typically learned about our limitations in niche subjects at a point in our lives when circumstances might have been less than ideal. We then proceeded to value, or rather devalue, ourselves accordingly. School subjects may seem varied to us in our prescriptive culture however, they are actually extremely limited. They mostly involve memorising or applying conventional thought processes. Whereas life and work require a range of other qualities, such as – leadership, emotional stability and intelligence, positivity, initiative, empathy, cooperative skills, creativity, resilience, resourcefulness and determination to name a few. We train and select people for many jobs based on academic performance, talking and appearances, when other factors are at least as important. The effectiveness of our caring professions requires considerable compassion and sensitivity, is this sufficiently nurtured/assessed? Many diverse aptitudes are inherent or lacking in individuals. Not detecting our natural skills, or trying to train them into people because of political pressure, can be highly inefficient. 'Horses for courses' is almost always better for everyone.

Only a fraction of what we are taught is used. At the same time, we fail to consider and build many necessary life and work skills. So why all the wasted effort and missed opportunities? Essentially, we have become so used to a narrow learning and assessment model that we fail to see beyond it. Our minds are entrenched in this mire which produces awkward societies and distorted lives. Most of us do, often unsuitable, routine tedious work using 'distractions' to ease the monotony while we worry about the future endlessly. The so called 'successful' think they have done well in the deal and invariably defend the system to the hilt, all the while wondering, 'Is this it?'

Understandably, those of us who think we have achieved some sort of success will favour whatever basis shows us in a good light because that offers much needed reassurance to our fragile, demanding egos. Unfortunately this normally provides only temporary respite from a shallow existence and it is not long before we are looking for 'more'. Restlessness and frustration, that continually seek fresh outlets, are the consequences as our unsatisfied minds try to deal with this makeshift mastery.

Underestimating

For decades I have heard people protest about losing jobs that can only be described as dreadful. They not only want to protect terrible work for themselves, but also for their children and grandchildren. These are fine people and I'm talking about really awful jobs here. That's how fearful and blinkered we have become; clinging to the most mind-numbing work in dire conditions at any cost. Loss of communities is a related fear often expressed. We seem to have forgotten that we are natural explorers, so creating new communities is a big part of the challenges we thrive on, or communities wouldn't have existed in the first place. When the time comes and the jobs go, there is doubtless some suffering. Then, after a few years, we find other ways to make a living and the majority of them are improvements if we are completely honest. Only the most rose-tinted sentimentality would see reasons to go back to anything resembling the relentless grind and toil previously defended so vehemently. Fear is a terrible thing. It is a real monster that gets it's claws deep inside us, our children and our children's children, if we let it. We defend the most irrational positions because for a time, long ago, they were all we had. Times change, and we can be our own worst enemies if we fail to realise this, grow up and tackle new challenges creatively. So where does this irrational fear and clinging come from which ignores our ability to ride most of life's storms? Childhood primarily, I suspect.

Aside from the importance of parenting, in a world of dependency where we subscribe to a system which labels us from our earliest years based on status, academic qualifications, surface impressions and other limited considerations, we eventually believe this is the whole story.

If we don't have the necessary credentials we are presumed to be 'inferior', and usually accept an undesirable future as our fathers and their fathers may have been forced to do (further testimony to how tradition and conditioned thinking can hold us back).

Talents

There is much more to us than recognised 'achievements' and appearances. Abilities come in all shapes and sizes. Our job is to look beyond social conditioning carefully and honestly, to find our most worthwhile aptitudes.

Ordinarily there is a trade-off in abilities, when we look closely. Extreme cases provide the best examples. Many 'geniuses' are renowned for their lack of common sense. 'Super-smart' savants can accomplish astonishing feats of memory, while they may be almost incapable of the simplest practical tasks. Seemingly there are people who cannot walk or talk but can sing and dance. Often numerical abilities come at the cost of language skills and vice-versa. The most talented entertainers are often the most exasperating characters – Prima Donnas. Some of us are good in teams, others operate better as individuals. Some follow instructions well, some are natural leaders. Huge muscle-bound men can hardly run whereas some small slim girls, with training, can jog along for hours. Physical or mental development may be earlier or later than expected. Early developers could expire sooner, while late developers can go on flowering well beyond most people. I think the point is clear – talent comes in several forms and many of the abilities we may regard as impressive have compensating downsides that aren't always apparent at first glance or from a distance.

On this point, I'm slightly sceptical about awards and accolades. Positive recognition does have a place, however if people are already benefiting from circumstances which have favoured their skills over others, do they deserve additional credit? Apart from that, they are very likely to have compensating inabilities, particularly if their talents are extreme. Like children we often admire extremes, oblivious to their downsides. Individuals with more balanced natures don't stand out generally although they tend to be more rounded agreeable people. We do what we can with the hand we have been dealt, so why fuss? Flattering egos is damaging. Fuelling mindsets of superiority or inferiority is divisive and detrimental to us all, even if we don't 'recognise' it.

It's worth considering further why we only appreciate a few of our abilities while probably possessing others that are buried. The reasons may be partly historical. For example, if certain talents could undermine the power or status of whoever influenced us, these abilities were liable to be dismissed or suppressed by those threatened, usually citing concern for the welfare of others as their justification. A few hundred years ago people were burned at the stake for 'witchcraft' because established hierarchies presumably saw certain valuable attributes as threatening. Apparently some 'witches' were capable of healing by simple hands-on methods. Related abilities with herbal cures are other key skills we have allowed to slip, creating a precarious reliance on commercialised medicines.

In other respects we may now be learning to take hidden talents a bit more seriously. Recent reports suggest modern official agencies have been researching telepathy and psychic aptitudes, with specific individuals producing consistently superior results. These speculative areas are very difficult to assess with our modern limited outlook. Who knows what wonders we may be capable of that were suppressed by medieval madness, and have yet to be unearthed in our world of money, micro-chips and mischief.

My core point is that, after millions of years of rigorous selection, passengers are unlikely to have survived. We could be talented in a multitude of different ways other than those commonly acknowledged. If we are sufficiently motivated or discontent, why not explore the possibility of possessing useful skills that escaped detection in earlier life, narrowing our options and holding us back.

Intelligent Thinking?

Definitions of intelligence vary. I have my own flexible ideas. Artificial intelligence is produced by a complex series of algorithms – on/off switches, and perhaps all intelligence boils down to that. Perhaps everything does!

Without thinking plants grow, flower, seed, fruit, deal with threats, take in water, nutrients and sunlight, and adapt to their environment. Over time their form, colour and design have combined in ways that help them survive. Similarly insects, birds and animals can instinctively find things, go places, communicate, cooperate, organise, raise offspring, settle disputes, avoid predators and so on without too much deliberating.

As for us, our prime functioning also has little to do with thinking. This includes – the blood that pumps through our veins; our appetites telling us to eat and drink or even what to eat and drink; our food that is digested and whose products are distributed where required in our bodies; our reproductive system with all the acquired information that is passed on, like how many legs and arms to grow, fingers and toes, eyes, ears, teeth, skin colour, hair type (all the relative positions and proportions of these features are guided by instructions contained in minute carrying devices and automatically transferred from generation to generation). Most of our everyday existence tasks are performed in this way without thinking, and they always have been. Human thinking is a very small and late player in the game of life so don't expect miracles... in that department anyway.

Human intelligent thinking employs our big brains, and we are frequently reminded by specialists how relatively large they are compared to other species. Then why do we get into so many difficulties? If you are anything like me you may have said to yourself innumerable times, 'If I'm so smart how come I'm in this mess, again?' It seems our brain power is deceptive. The truth is, we are not all that clever. After millennia spent principally hunting and exploring we suddenly expect our brains to master universally ideal solutions, which remain elusive... unsurprisingly.

Faculties

The human brain may look advanced in comparison to mice or even chimpanzee brains but it is no hot shot. It's a tool that formed to help us survive, reproduce and diversify. Inter-galactic travel or turning-back time have never been at the top of our priority list, and our brain has a lot to do with priorities. It does certain things far better than other creatures although these skills are, to a great extent, 'trying to make a silk purse out of a sow's ear'. The quality of information human senses can send to our brains is fairly rudimentary when compared to certain animals. Our sense of smell is woeful in comparison to dogs, cats, deer, bears, lions, tigers or pigs, for a start. Our hearing is nowhere near the best, and our eyesight is limited in colour spectrum, distance and flexibility, compared to various 'dumb things'.

Yes, some creatures do fare worse than humans when it comes to specific senses however they usually compensate in other departments. Bats, for instance, use sonar devices we can only marvel at that allow them to operate at night yet avoid bumping into one another, as they travel at super-slick speeds in densely congested throngs of thousands. Sharks have sensors to detect the electro-magnetic fields given off by other life forms, and possess sophisticated filtering systems which pick-up occurrences across miles of vast seas.

Physically, the story doesn't get much better for humans. We're not very fast, not very strong and not very durable by big animal standards. Are we a jack of all trades, master of none? The indications are – we *need* those bigger brains to offset our limitations and allow us to compete.

The Ultimate Test

Despite their skills and attributes other creatures can be prone to suicidal overindulgence. Some know how to make the most of what is available, whereas several won't stop till they drop (a trait we often mirror). They exhaust their environment and pay the ultimate price for this lack of foresight. They are also susceptible to changed circumstances that tax them beyond their limits. A few manage to muster sufficient self-preserving adaptability but many are not so lucky.

Fortunately we *are* adaptable, and succumbing to short-sightedness is something we're capable of improving on if we choose to. In spite of our drawbacks, when we compare humans to other life forms, we appear to be a very capable bunch if the notion takes us. We create powerful tools; we can plan and organise well; we keep vast detailed information records; we can conduct complex large-scale experiments; we are highly sociable (surprisingly enough); and we can occasionally think things through before acting; but we're not out of the woods yet...

Human numbers have grown from 2 billion to 7 billion in the last 80 years, after centuries of relative population stability involving losses caused by disease, war and other catastrophes followed by gradual replenishment. It now looks like we are on an exponentially accelerating course with our big brains leading the way. Significant scientific advances have contributed greatly to these mammoth population increases and created an entirely new set of quandaries for us to resolve.

We are a relatively recent species that has already managed to produce this unsustainable population growth together with the means to eradicate ourselves and most of our unsuspecting companions. Conceivably the 'experiment' of human life has a not too distant expiry date.

Hence the overriding need to probe what it is about us that creates so many problems when we have such big brains.

Let's face it, our numerous improvements haven't exactly made life a bowl of cherries so far, to be honest. Could we be misusing our brains? Maybe we haven't mastered their power. How much do our emotions get in the way, and what can we do to improve?

Thankfully, more than any other species, we have the capability to anticipate, consider and modify outcomes. Understanding how we misuse our brains' mechanisms and the consequences can help. On top of childhood influences and fear based egos continually tripping us up, our current combination of tight overstimulation with blinkered thinking makes us try to run before we can walk and build without proper foundations. Our predominant 'work/play trap' omits a key individual growth element, essential for healthy balanced living and responsible progress. We are struggling to master driving our vehicle on all four wheels – Work, Play, Relax and Grow, making the ride bumpy at best. This molotov cocktail isn't helped by underutilising our skills. Without fuller appreciation and employment of our abilities, we will surely suffer more than necessary.

Ultimately, any species failing to use it's expensively acquired range of talents sensibly is taking unnecessarily high risks in the survival game.

Judge mental

Lately I've become aware of myself and almost everyone around me being unnecessarily judgemental, as if we have exclusivity on correctness, and the world should conform to our requirements. It is so present every minute of every day in many of us that we take it for granted. This is the children's world of good and bad, right and wrong, heroes and villains, entitlement and expectation.

Talking about others and their faults is a national pastime. Expecting apologies, blaming and criticising, because we are perfect and others aren't. Is this really true? What gives us the right to expect perfection in people when we can't or won't see our own imperfections? When we condemn and criticise people who don't do what suits *us* we fuel fear, create barriers and reduce cooperation. At the same time we display our lack of understanding for all to see. Condemnation and criticism are forms of negativity, and negativity damages everyone involved. Protection, correction or avoidance may be sensible but easy criticism, rather than closer consideration, ironically harms ourselves by reinforcing limiting perspectives.

A friend once told me, 'Yes you are unique, just like everyone else.' We thrive on healthy diversity. Everyone has what we call, a distinct personality. That means everyone has a different, if similar, design. Hardly surprising then, we think and act differently sometimes. In fact, the real surprise is how uniform we manage to be.

As if oblivious to the above, we often treat people worse than machines, plants or animals. If people say or do something we don't agree with, we condemn them. If we have problems with a machine or anything else, we seek the fault or cause. However when it comes to other folk we overlook the fact that people are, in essence, complex machines. Like machines, people are 'made', and our complexity creates a mass of opportunities for functioning fluctuations, some of them considerable. Do we kick a car if it won't start? I know we want to but do we also want a huge bodywork repair bill when all we really need is a jump-start? Has the car been treated well and are our expectations reasonable? Maybe not, and that is often the case with our expectations of people when we look beyond our first reaction, which is usually to criticise.

The love/hate flip-flop is a trait of children that reveals their underdeveloped reasoning. If you do what they want they love you, if not, they hate you. This is how many of us continue to deal with the world as adults, and demonstrates our psychological immaturity. Remember a small child wants to believe it is the centre of the universe and expects everything to revolve around him or her. Although ultimately gratifying, the pressing transition to a more sophisticated reality can be painful and is avoided if at all possible. This necessitates progressively convoluted detours and denial in adulthood.

Complaining, criticising, demanding, frustration, anger and expectation are all valid on occasions. Unchecked, these tendencies with their accompanying negative emotions are draining. They are often habits based on childhood fears and helplessness. It's a pity we didn't learn to gladly fend for ourselves as required rather than continually complaining as we go, or waiting for someone to provide for us. So we remain stuck, condemning and attempting to make the world comply with our 'rightful' demands.

Judgers

We are regularly judged from an early age. At school, in sports, in competitions, or by our friends and families. Later, some of us even seek out being judged for the familiarity of it, while remaining oblivious to this and the harm it does. (A high level of self-consciousness, even vanity, is common in people accustomed to being excessively judged.)

Judging is popular in the media. They know how to press our buttons. TV talent shows (or 'no talent' shows) and contests abound, where people are constantly judged. Political debates, celebrity lifestyles, critical sports analyses, how people dress, what they say, how they live, how they drive, what the inside of their homes look like, their hobbies and so on. 'Who do you blame?' 'Who's fault was it?' 'You know you are entitled to compensation for their mistakes.' There are theatre critics, music critics, wine critics, food critics, critics, critics, critics. There will soon be university courses on criticism and blame, if they don't already exist. Here *I* am criticising. It lures you into it's web.

We share our complaints with friends – no sooner has the weather been sufficiently maligned, than we let them know who or what we have been inconvenienced by or dismayed at. We complain on TV, radio, the phone, in the press, by form or letter and especially in complainers heaven – the internet. An ideal spot to be busy doing nothing, just complaining. Complaining is more about talk than action. Telling others what to do or not to do, rather than doing much about anything ourselves. It is a common trademark of bullies, and bullies are essentially frightened people trying to feel more powerful, or less inadequate. In person, complaining could get a bit tricky. We might have to worry about offending someone and the repercussions, like being told to examine our own lives more carefully. 'No, that requires a degree of maturity and some sense of responsibility that I can't be bothered acquiring. I'd rather be a dictator on the internet. That's the safest place for me, Mr Scared and Angry.'

Other Sources & Solutions

Apart from offering a valuable excuse to be lazy and demanding, being judgemental provides another veiled strategy to compensate for our personal insecurities. By criticising others we put them down. This effectively raises our relative standing with minimum effort, particularly when we create a one-way dialogue. Being the boss, a parent or part of an advantaged group against weaker opponents can reduce the chances of any unwelcome rebuff from our target, and hopefully give us the coveted last word. Of course, nothing works better than the private conversations in our head which condemn the 'inadequates' and reassure us of our superiority. We are now well down that slippery slope of self-delusion on the rocky road to nowhere.

An example of widespread dismissal of others, aimed at giving us a feeling of superiority, is our modern glib tendency to refer to senior political figures by their surnames. What was intended as a pseudo-slick journalistic technique has become a poorly camouflaged form of abuse. We may not agree with their actions, approaches or even principles still, the work of political leaders far exceeds what most of us would undertake. They certainly require careful monitoring but disrespecting those who willingly tackle some of society's most demanding challenges demonstrates divisive attitudes rooted in judgemental conditioning.

Like many other negative traits, being judgemental is a clumsy, fear-based, survival mechanism. It is a means of telling ourselves, and anyone who will listen, that we are more entitled to be accommodated (have our needs met and therefore survive) than other people. Fear may be useful periodically although it's persistent presence, aided by adopting a multitude of distracting disguises, can make life arduous. It naturally triggers physiological changes in our body chemistry which can only be sustained temporarily without damage. Too much fear, too much negativity, and it won't be long before our worst fears really *do* materialise.

We typically acquire judgemental behaviour from strong influences such as parents. Their actions or words showed us how things 'should be' and we absorbed much of their style, if not values necessarily. Whatever the manifestations, being judgemental is a debilitating tactic we have mostly copied inadvertently. The saddest effect is when we make our lives overly burdensome by all too frequently judging ourselves even *more* harshly than we judge others.

Being habitually judgemental creates obstacles and complications until we recognise it. When we do, the traps are exposed so we can try to avoid them with a little care, making living more forgiving.

Good Judgement

There is a world of difference between being judgemental and exercising good judgement. One is a damaging waste of energy, the other is crucial.

A wise man was asked how to find happiness.
'Good judgement,' was his reply.

He was then asked how to obtain this good judgement.
'Experience,' he added.

He was finally asked how to gain the required experience.
'Bad judgement,' he concluded with a smile.

We all need to make choices in life and the better our choices, the better our lives. Good judgement can be hard to acquire, especially if we were domineered, confused or spoiled by our parents. (Take your pick, few are exempt.) These encounters stunt our progress, making choices tough and scary. What then follows is a lacklustre repetitive cycle of rehashing tired solutions, repeating familiar habits and only making well-tried and tested decisions or variations of them. Avoiding completely fresh situations with their inevitable new choice requirements becomes our norm, and accordingly we stay stuck.

As the wise man said, good judgement requires exploration and a willingness to accept mistakes, more aptly termed lessons, as an integral part of the discovery process. It's not about knowing outcomes before we try, that's predictability which quickly turns into a dull strategy.

Yes, awareness of our changing limits *is* important. Nonetheless, a vital ingredient for improving life is the determination to follow exploring instincts. That requires our resourcefulness to be exercised by spotting outdated self-imposed boundaries, and *judiciously* crossing them from time to time.

Separation

A Psychologist once told me, 'It's not Psychology, its life,' and he was right. No matter what label we use to describe any subject they are all parts of life, categorised by humans for 'convenience'. Our tendency to forget this, or failure to see the connections, can leave us stranded.

Imagine a herd of elephants casually tramping through the jungle (bear with me here). One swelteringly hot day, the big boss has a brainwave and suggests they each focus on more specialist roles like food, defence, navigation or kids. To enable this, they could reduce their involvement in other areas. After a bit of trumpeting and bumping around nothing much can be agreed, so they saunter along steadily much the same as before and continue to do whatever elephants do. Humans are smarter than elephants though (or anything else of course). We *did* manage to split life into more specific tasks and territories. A measure of separation was helpful but we exaggerated our divisions under labels like – Nations, Science, Religion, Law, Economics, Entertainment, Politics et al. Unlike our elephants, who stayed true to their broad-based elephant nature, we humans got pigeon-holed by this arrangement. We saw life through human labels and overlooked that everything is intrinsically the same natural process or processes, with or without human categories and interpretations. We also created lines of demarcation with hierarchies where outsiders feared to tread, resulting in isolated thinking. To the untrained eye this looked progressive, so the many followed the few –

'In the land of the blind, the one eyed man is king.'

That's how smart people like us ended up muddled. We separated into sectors for 'efficiency' and order, became something more specific and forgot how to be all we are. Breeding and cultures extended many of the divides, then before we knew it we were straightjacketing ourselves and arguing with each other from dissociated viewpoints. What a not so wise bunch we have turned into, through labelling and separating life.

Away With Words

A few thousand years ago humans developed language. Therefore it is another relatively recent device, and now we fail to appreciate how much the array of assumptions, shortcuts and detours it produces constrain us.

Wanting Words

If we became seriously ill or lost someone close; if we won the lottery or just had a child; if we were reunited with a long lost friend or saw harrowing scenes of suffering and were asked to explain how we felt, it would be hard to find the right words, in fact it would be impossible. We scream, we cry, we gasp, we sigh because words are not enough. Touch, sights, sounds, tastes, smells, and feelings involve so much more than words could ever describe. Music bypasses language to impart sublime 'messages', making it both strange and amusing to hear music being analysed at length with words. Still, we place considerable importance on words and frequently rely on them totally.

Words cause confusion when they are expected to provide explanations beyond their capabilities. Furthermore, misplaced, mistimed, inadequate or inappropriate words can get us into all kinds of bother. Some words mean different things at different times to different people. We talk about justice when we often mean revenge. Love is another good example. We can love our children or our partner or our new shoes. So what is this love? There are dictionary definitions of words and slang meanings. There are historical interpretations of words which clash completely with modern usage. Merely translating from one language to another can trip us because certain languages contain concise depictions that don't exist in others, we have to use approximations and the intended meaning is distorted or lost.

I have a friend with a stammer who had difficulty saying the words he wanted to at times, and could only force out other words in desperation. As you can imagine, this was not just painfully frustrating for him, it could confuse matters entirely. Words regularly create, less apparent, similar snags across the board.

We live in a society increasingly based on words which have their uses but restrict our understanding if we don't look past them. I am using words to communicate now and they paint just a partial picture. If you could see and hear me (relax, it's not compulsory) my delivery would be more complete though subject to our interaction at the time. Seemingly, in 'face to face' conversations, less than 10 percent of the meaning is derived from the words used, and nearly 40 percent comes from the voice tone or inflection, with over 50 percent contributed by other context elements such as body language. I doubt if this is the whole story, however one thing *is* clear – words play a supporting role to many other factors. (Where does that leave texting, emails, websites… and books like this?)

Missing Out

It isn't accurate to say, 'This is a – river, star, dog, flower, Scandinavian,' or anything. A word, label or description is not what something actually *is*. We are using shortcuts. If

I write the word 'sunset or ocean' and proceed to portray them in a million words, you will never comprehend how it feels to enjoy a sunset or an ocean up close; in the flesh so to speak. We need to experience things in person to unwrap their substance, not via words.

We categorise then sub-divide in great detail and assume we know. What is a bird? Each one is unique and promises a novel encounter depending on the context. In order to communicate with other humans we use the label 'bird' to generally describe something with feathers (more human labels) that flies (more human labels). Birds were around long before us so what were they then, without our collective terms? Next we group similar life types and call them 'species' to assist human differentiation. This mainstream identification method conditions our attitudes towards them, which is unfortunate as it offers a decidedly incomplete appreciation.

If we want to get somewhere quickly we take the shortest route; but if we want to savour the view or the atmosphere, and feel invigorated, we take the scenic path. We may even stop to 'stretch our legs', 'inhale the air', 'listen to the birds', 'paddle in the water' or 'take in the sunset'. Are you getting the picture? The words are less than a glimpse. Their best efforts cannot approach the fuller, real, connecting, flowing event that arises when we go beyond words to take in realness.

Descriptions don't supply shortcuts solely. They can also take us on the most fanciful detours. European politicians recently spent years debating definitions of chocolate. Words were important for their political and administrative purposes yet, as we very much appreciate, chocolate is all about the taste not any description.

Tribal Territory

Land is divided into 'countries' on pieces of paper (which change as required from time to time) and given names for practicality. Then, we 'belong' to these countries which were simply designated and labelled by someone. We see the labelled country as part of our self, and look for things to be proud of or upset by which relate to *our* country. We dig back in time to find long-lost ancestors, cultures, heroes or injustices to revisit and even re-invent. We admire *our* country's open vistas, heartened, as if they somehow stimulate a fabricated sense of personal specialness, as much as affinity. All the time we are taken for a ride by words and labels that humans just constructed to classify and manage areas. Tribal traits are evident as we automatically attach to something that was devised for order, and are affronted at the mere suggestion this could all be a hollow contrivance. We wave flags, resent others and 'loyally' support competitors who represent our 'country'. Words attributed to George Bernard Shaw entertainingly capture the selective rationale we employ...

> *'Patriotism is the belief that our country is better than any other because we were born in it.'*

Don't get me wrong, I'm all for some sense of belonging and locals dealing with local issues where it works. Cultures give us something of 'our own' to develop using the positive aspects of our tribal nature. Their diversity can teach us a lot and encourage a broad range of paths. What I'm wary of are the disguised personal insecurities and superficial assumptions that foster small-minded parochialism leading to resentment, stagnation and all too often unnecessary conflict.

Clichés

Descriptions, communication and real progress require a range of language, as cooking requires a range of ingredients to avoid unappetising meals. I may not be the best illustration of this, with my literary limitations, but I'm trying. That's the point, trying.

We use 'trendy' clichés, originally favoured by youth to impress, and adopted by many to appear hip, such as – 'Cool. Cool. Cool. Wicked!' or 'Hey guys. You guys. Thanks guys. Hi guys.' There are business clichés designed to sound slick like – 'Out of the box. Ticking all the boxes. In the zone. Head hunted. On or off the radar.' We readily resort to superlatives (often products of child psyche) for anything resembling a different or enjoyable experience – 'Brilliant! Amazing! Awesome! Fantastic!' Then there are our continual nervous insertions of superfluous pause words – 'I was like, she was like, he was like,' or 'You know, you know, you know.' Highlighting our slide in sophistication, the use of swearing for effect is now routine in entertainment. Most of us succumb to clichés from time to time. They are lazy thinking and add to a 'more of the same' existence. Words and phrases are picked up from seeing and hearing, repetition breeds habit and habit affects our growth and gratification.

In a related vein, there is a popular saying that warns…

> *'Be careful of your thoughts, as they will become your words.*
> *Be careful of your words, as they will become your actions.*
> *Be careful of your actions, as they will become your habits.*
> *Be careful of your habits, as they will become your character.*
> *Be careful of your character, as it will become your destiny.'*
>
> …ANONYMOUS.

Assumptions

Questions are the means to answers, and asking the right questions helps us to find the best answers. Conversely, asking loaded questions containing presumptions straightjackets our answers and our world. A classic example is the television interviewer who says, 'So who is to blame?' As if we are children intent on abdicating responsibility by blaming others, rather than adults searching for the wider correctable causes in which we all have a duty of care. Or, 'What is your favourite... whatever?' I enjoy different things at different times, why should I be limited by a favourite? Maybe I do have a favourite but it could change any time, and favourites aren't compulsory.

This reminds me of the wonderful reply I heard from an African football fan who transcended the loaded question, 'Who do you support?'... 'I support football! I support football!' he jubilantly yelled. A truly liberating answer that definitely made me tingle.

We label ourselves and everything, then see the world as we think it is based on our conditioned view of these labels. There is one blind assumption after another here, keeping us pinned down while life flows. If we feel stuck, it's time to see beyond common labels and concepts. This frees us to find fitting assessments in every changing situation, using all our faculties. As the renowned architect Charles Rennie Mackintosh stated –

'Don't meddle with other people's ideas when you have your work cut out for you in trying to express your own. Shake off all the props that tradition and authority offer you and go alone. Crawl, stumble, stagger but go alone.'

Have we lost our appetite for this, or is it merely dormant?

Religion

A controversial area if ever there was one, that deserves respect. We all expect to be treated reasonably and feel insulted when we are not. Religion lies at the centre of many lives and therefore deserves the respect we all value for what is important to us.

Religion, more than any other subject, is separated and debated fruitlessly ad-infinitum, when it could be more productively considered collectively as a part of human behaviour. Religion is a reflection of what we are or think we are, or have been told to think we are. When we say harm is done by Religion, we are actually saying that harm is done by people, in the name of Religion. As we know, people do both harm and good in the name of countless causes, and we use Religion similarly. It is the make-up of *people* which is the underexposed source of many issues, at least as much as the make-up of religions.

Religions may subscribe to the simplified polarities of good and bad or right and wrong but, if we investigate, they allude to hidden depths. Beneath their creative interpretations, our main religions could be said to have evolved from variations of the same messages, and that is possibly a clue to their survival and relevance. However, when we rely on the proclamations of others who have a vested interest in our deference, they are unlikely to provide us with many liberating concepts.

Nonetheless, religions must have some sound bases and strike chords with people or they would have died long ago. That said, they assume a power exceeding their intention when we unwittingly use them to fill an identity gap in our lives.

In The Beginning

Centuries ago, few people were educated and societies had only reached an early stage when religions appeared. Medicine could not do much for the sick, and food supplies were subject to weather, pests and other threats. Also, people lacked our modern means to enforce law and order. In this climate of susceptibility and simplicity, beliefs based on some type of judgemental father figure could be tied-in with life experiences, to an extent. A sort of alpha-male domination could still be seen at the head of families, tribes and societies, additionally inclining us towards the idea of a figurehead superior to ourselves. When you are struggling to survive and everyone around you follows similar beliefs, falling in line can be the best policy, especially when an ideology is tailored to suit your context. In this climate, religions could take hold and some flourished.

Our childhood and pack mentality predispose us to a sort of intimidation and subservient admiration of whatever represents 'status', like – gods, celebrities, wealth and prestige. Many modern staged events offer the opportunity to pay homage and we gladly oblige. When enough humans put anything on a pedestal, multitudes will follow.

Preaching Practicality

In a world with little structure, Religion helped to convey 'mutually beneficial' advice from the wise few who could see further, to the useful many who were busy with their heads down. As religions caught-on and grew, they became formidable. Mighty hierarchies arose together with elaborate costumes and ceremonies which enforced their position. Ornate temples of worship were built to accommodate followers and encourage respect. Some were necessarily huge, overawing people and adding to the intimidation. The old useful advice was embellished for effect using 'Holy' rituals, enshrining it in mystique that contributed to conformity long after it's true relevance had expired. Nowadays ancient terms and language add gravitas, strengthening the 'ultimate source' notion.

To see past our assumptions of Divine instruction, it's worth examining religious rites with an open mind for their likely original man-made practical intentions. These are only a few illustrations of the many possibilities –

Fasting

Prepared us to cope with food shortages and rested our digestion. It created a healthy discipline, allowing us to appreciate and enjoy our food more. Today, much religious fasting has succumbed to evasive compromises diluting it's value, usually because most people are simply following rather than understanding. Moderation is something we now acknowledge the value of, even if we don't always manage to achieve our worthy aims.

Food

Eating certain animals in ancient times in hot climates posed a major health risk so it was presumably restricted or forbidden. Also, in spite of the temptation to consume them as soon as folk got hungry, some animals had to be retained so they were protected by decree. Caution with food is still important although modern facilities reduce many risks (and create a few of their own).

Footwear
Shoes were taken off before going indoors, keeping dirt at bay and preventing diseases being passed on, particularly when there were large gatherings without modern sanitation. We are more concerned about our clean carpets and comfort these days, nevertheless the hygiene logic of removing or changing footwear indoors remains sound.

Clothing
Head-dresses can add status, protect, show conformity and aid hygiene. Depending on the situation, it can make sense to add or remove head-dresses. Covering up women avoided men being easily distracted in large communities. This could protect women, help to reduce social tensions and increase productivity.

Ceremonies
Provide reassurance to individuals and societies as well as encouraging respect for key stages of life. They also help to keep Religion at the centre of people's lives, which would originally have been intended for our welfare. Births, deaths and marriages are significant milestones in any life, so influence here is powerful.

Worship & Prayer
Apart from unhealthy religious subjugation and enforced conformity, genuine humility associated with prayer is a deft device to bypass ego. The accompanying silent contemplation can also calm the mind.

Sabbath
Provided a therapeutic break for rest and reflection.

Religious customs and rituals are too numerous to mention. We can enjoy examining any that are of special interest to ourselves. Most of them probably had practical significance in the absence of anything better at the time. In some cases, better options were possibly suppressed by authority.

In modern merging societies we should take into account humans are naturally territorial, and it is helpful to recognise that overt 'symbolism', religious or otherwise, used outside accepted territories can seem threatening or challenging to others. This makes cooperation and integration more awkward, no matter how tolerant we 'ought' to be.

Bold Beliefs

As humans, ultimately our real needs are similar, even if what we *want* has been shaped very differently. It is up to us to unblock the paths in our hearts and minds that enable us to move forward effectively. This takes courage, questioning and humility for a start.

If someone applies for a job we expect to see evidence of their aptitude – qualifications, references, tests, presentations, demonstrations, anything we can assess before we decide. When we are asked to accept something that cannot be proved or disproved, that no one can experience and report back on, which seems far fetched and we are expected to commit our entire lives to, it would be wise to err on the side of caution. The only sane reasons for subscribing to highly speculative concepts are that – we *want to*, or are afraid not to. Many religions use 'life after death' as the big pull, and what could be more convenient. It can neither be proved or disproved, and people really want to believe it. That is the draw. Humans are emotionally led, marvellous at seeing what we want to see and closing our eyes to inconvenient obstacles, like absent evidence.

Could stories of 'life after death', with their associations of repentance, resurrection and Heaven, be some of our 'key' misinterpretations? Are they actually simplified texts to aid our understanding? What if they represent giving up a life of fixed ideas for a life of seeing everything freshly as it emerges, with the advantages that accompany such an approach. How much could we have 'wasted' by taking messages like these too literally?

Bearing that in mind, it's worth considering what is meant and conveyed by the term 'God'. This ordinarily conjures up the image of a wise old man with a white beard in a place called Heaven, or something of that ilk. I would suggest a more complete idea of God is that which lies outwith our imagination or comprehension, rendering any concept or image a contradiction. The label 'God' might be used to symbolise unknown powers and forces affecting or controlling our lives. That patchy impression could be helpful because these forces deserve respect, as long as the respect doesn't prevent us questioning. If some are happy to stop learning about life's exciting mysteries by labelling them 'God', that's fine. Natural curiosity will take many of us further, as we attempt to discover and enjoy what lies beyond the boundaries of traditional thinking.

Is God a verb rather than a noun?

Seeing ourselves as part of God rather than something separate might be a good idea; after all, if God is everything we are clearly included in that. Intriguingly, we are told, 'God is love', making my upcoming section on Love potentially pivotal. Meanwhile, anyone who sees God as a father figure should bear in mind that the prime purpose of an effective father is sometimes described as – teaching us how to flourish without a father.

What if Religion was entirely created by humans? Every word, belief and temple, a human construct. This is only an obstacle when denied; whereas if we accept humans set it up, we can then enhance it. Stripping away bygone terms, concepts and, most of all, interpretations which no longer apply, might reveal very pertinent wisdom.

Wise leaders don't encourage dogma, with the shackles that partner it. They promote cooperation irrespective of their ideologies, anticipating the benefits this can yield. They realise we are all in the same team playing the same game, and they work tirelessly towards a constructive climate. (Those who do otherwise are treating their followers like children and missing the point, surely.) This is the domain of peaceful contemplation, free thinking and prudent action that transcends fear based ideals steeped in the past.

Misunderstood Religion has complicated and confused mankind's intentions for centuries with it's seductive promises of eternal salvation elsewhere, in return for blind faith and deference here and now. This is a diversion that causes us to underutilise our more immediate potential. Realising the worth in 'life before death' may be the underlying message of Religion, and a very tangible one at that.

Hidden Treasure

Dig deep enough into many religions and you will find gold, real gold. Not the gold you can spend, the gold of insight that transforms lives. Disappointingly, some religious leaders are too preoccupied with worship and obedience to search for the freedoms religions were founded upon; that bold dedicated sages so painstakingly experienced, analysed and attempted to pass-on many moons ago. Yes, some religious teachers *do* try their best to shed more light on things but several simply continue to teach as they were taught, while others are more concerned with status or power (they're only human after all). Essentially ceremonies, theological debates and concerns about threats obscure the bigger picture. They conceal and distract from the precious core wisdom at the heart of human understanding, containing the secrets of alchemy. Yes… Alchemy! Alchemy is not actually about transforming base metal into gold, as myth implies. It's about transforming lives. Turning a mundane existence into something enjoyable and gratifying. This is the liberating power we all hold in our hands right now. Countless 'intellectuals' routinely dismiss Religion without seeking the treasure behind the label. The baby is being thrown out with the bathwater, as we swap 'Divine' indoctrination for our modern replacements.

The 'Spiritual' aspect within Religion is where the big lessons can be learned. These are lessons about not simply following. Lessons about 'growing up'. Lessons about not requiring others to interpret for us. Lessons about recognising when our beliefs have us trapped and are contributing to our trials and tribulations. Lessons about grasping that most religions were based on teachings devised to help ALL people, and that religious conflict confuses and hinders everyone. Of course we can stand up for our values when pressured or threatened although that would also be better founded on adequately considered reasoning rather than dogmatic emotional ideology.

Religion attempts to articulate what we thought we knew about how to live contentedly, yet it produces no shortage of stern faces and intense attitudes. Is this the price we pay for following prescriptive beliefs – division, deference, and sacrificing a light heart for a heavy one? We frequently fail to spot that one of the fundamental messages of Religion is FREEDOM (with it's responsibilities), and so end up living in the shadows of some decreed view.

Who is truly responsible for the restrictions anyway? Could it be ourselves? How did we find Religion? Did we inherit it from our family or culture? Were we spoon-fed it and brainwashed into submission? Are we looking for easy answers to bespoke quandaries that really require more personal searching? Do we need reassurance, or to belong, or to fill a gap in our lives? These are all valid means of discovery but what have we learned for *ourselves*? Do our beliefs free us to thrive or have we just traded one type of confinement for another?

Religion *can* show us the way, perhaps more than many other methods. However, it is only a means to an end, not an end in itself. It's answers often point towards bigger questions, and that's life.

When we do our own digging, we will know without question if we strike *real* 'GOLD' via Religion or otherwise. That's when the unnecessary struggles we continually create in our minds subside, albeit intermittently, and are replaced by a fresh, uplifting awareness.

Money

Let's round off our tour of modern life's most misleading muddles by visiting the daddy of them all. The place where most of us head, given half a chance. Money is another adult equivalent of sweets to a child. When our goal is money and we expect it to be a panacea, we are again falling for surface impressions.

Money makes the world go round. Yes, round and round till our heads are spinning and we don't know where we are or where we're going, except to search for more. Money turns into a problem when underdeveloped thinking perpetually sees it as the prime goal. If our parents held money in high regard (for their own reasons), we often automatically give it a central role, unless we are fortunate enough to question their values. Money is certainly useful, so what is the flip-side? How can money make us sick? How can a rich man gain the world and lose his soul, as the old saying warns? To understand, we need to clarify a few additional things about life... and money.

Money Matters

If we go back in our trusty time machine, we see our ancestors living mainly from day to day. Their level of happiness is debatable, still, they were used to this and adapting accordingly. Realising it would be helpful to plan for a rainy day, they stored some food and other useful items whenever possible. Any surplus could be traded if a suitable opportunity arose. So far so good. Then various forms of money appeared, as trading and societies got more sophisticated. That's money – we do our work and use money to exchange surpluses by trading. Fine. No harm in that then? Not until some of us get greedy. Money is a tool in the the age old game of resource allocation. Like children, instead of sharing we often want to keep more because we 'need' more or it 'belongs' to us; we 'found' it – finders keepers. If only life was that simple and people readily submitted to claims of greater entitlement. Watch what happens when animals get greedy with each other – tyranny or trouble, or both! Surprisingly humans aren't much different. Failure to share and cooperate wisely has fuelled the destructive fires of division which exist in almost every society and between societies. Claiming our 'entitlements' are paramount, has led us into numerous costly conflicts. (How's that for a potted history of global economics.)

In a nutshell – surplus leads to trading, and trading can be abused (or disregarded completely by the unethical) leading to conflict. Throughout history we have fought to claim or protect 'surpluses', which often merely served to compound our excesses. We boast of historical conquests and admire their legacies of ornate buildings, social systems, infra-structure, monuments, what we call 'treasures', and extensive modified landscapes. Some are useful or interesting, many are simply testimony to our indulgences. More recently, we have created economies and lifestyles based on consuming what we don't need, or even what is harmful to us. Global industries have been built on the premise that it is important to convince us we *do* need all this dubious stuff. Advancement becomes a by-product, accompanied by distorted circumstances and the enormous social costs of this arrangement. Everyone is afraid to let go of the cycle, fearing catastrophe. As individuals (and consequently societies) we don't seem to be capable of balancing worthwhile activities with the not so worthwhile, and basing our lives correspondingly. Therefore we pay the price till we learn. Maybe the fundamentals aren't perceived, or we won't believe in our ability to upgrade until we are forced to. Better work, better relationships, better lifestyles, better conditions and smoother progress all await us recognising the obsolescence of what has led us here, and the steps we can take to improve.

Enough Is As Good As A Feast

In modern society our essential needs are reasonably attainable, on the whole. Anything else is a bonus and surely we would be foolish to constantly struggle for more, but many do. Why? Remember our scurrilous tempter The Child Catcher. We see bigger, brighter, 'better' things and we want them or feel left out. The child in us wants more and hasn't been shown any other route so we march along to someone else's tune for the sake of 'more'. Our insecurities seek status and prestige to demonstrate our 'importance' so we roll up our sleeves and plunge into the lifelong quest for security or 'success'. We are running in a race we cannot win, although somehow we can't afford to lose. All the time our head is down, missing heaps, because we want to get somewhere 'better', usually in a hurry, but where exactly?

We don't know when enough is enough, just like – the child in the sweet shop eating till it is sick, or Ebeneezer Scrooge being obsessed with money and forgetting how to live happily. Both arise mostly from limited perspectives leading to unhealthy overindulgences and fears of losing-out. When our only philosophy is 'more is better', our appetites are insatiable and our mindset is narrow.

We compare ourselves to others around us which is natural, and healthy up to a point. Alas, that point has been well exceeded by our population concentrations and common media messages. Without wisdom, the race goes on and on. We settle into a groove of continuous demand and consumption, or we grow sickened and begin to look for other ways, if we're lucky.

Reconsidering the basis of our assumptions about money and understanding ourselves better *might* help. Money is neither the core problem, nor the solution to our happiness. Evidently, our levels of happiness are only temporarily increased by large amounts of money. I'm not in line with most measures of 'happiness' but there is a message here. Money doesn't remove basic insecurity, it only relieves financial insecurities until the inevitable worries about any type of loss or insufficiency re-emerge. Money worshipers and continual status seekers usually find something to reignite their fears fairly quickly, regardless of what they achieve. Money doesn't provide freedom, it provides apparent financial freedom that ties us to a life of money *matters*. It may seem ideal to those of us who have little, or that see life as a prestige contest; however it doesn't change us inside for very long. Why? Because we can change *how* we are (partly) but we can't change *what* we are.

Our nature is key, so it's worth considering – if left alone, would a tree fare better inside a palace or in a modest garden?

There is a well known poem by William Henry Davies called
Leisure, written long ago when times were far more difficult
for most people than they are today. It starts –

> 'What is this life if full of care,
> we have no time to stand and stare.
> No time to stand beneath the boughs
> and stare as long as sheep or cows…'

I'll leave you to enjoy the rest some other time. Anyway,
I expect you're thinking that this poet lived a privileged
existence, being able to indulge in poetry and staring like
cows in times of hardship for many. Well, not really. In fact,
for a significant part of his life, William Henry Davies was,
believe it or not, a vagabond! Yes, a tramp. How could he live
like this in these tough times and write such touching words?
Did he realise something we don't about life, and money?

LOST Exit

It doesn't take much for our little boats to run aground in the murky waters of day to day life which conceal a collection of catches like – dated influences, egos, moods, distractions and a host of misunderstandings that steer us into lost living. The inevitable worry, self-doubt, and confusion created further complicates our journey as we repeatedly bump into the world in this darkness.

OK, now the hazards have been revealed we can alter our course and make some long overdue progress, can't we?

I wish!

The reality is, most of us prefer to keep our eyes closed or stay put. We don't want to give up whatever it is we have for the sake of some pie in the sky 'freedom' unless we are forced to. The regular routine is familiar so why not just persevere with it?

> There was once a bird who lived in a feeble bare tree. It was the only tree around, so he stayed close to protect his perch. One day a huge gust of wind blew his frail tree away, forcing him to fly over the hill. There, to his amazement, he discovered flocks of friendly birds just like him and a lush forest of strong healthy trees where he thrived.

In truth, the main things we ought to give up are old fears, attitudes and fixed ideas that hamper us. Maybe then we'll find that the culmination of our life's adventure isn't too far away after all.

FOUND

After years of being lost, something is changing. A breeze is taking us out of the shallows into more open water. The mist is beginning to lift and we can see more clearly. This brings a fresh sense of anticipation, accompanied by doubts such as – do we really want to be intrepid explorers or are we home-birds getting out of our depth? Perhaps we should turn around, go back. Who knows what risks we might be taking?

…or what exhilarating escapades beckon? Nothing ventured nothing gained, as they say. We've come this far so let's see what we're made of, and if there really are surprises to be enjoyed waiting for us around the corner.

Foundations

Any builder will tell you the importance of proper foundations. The better they are, the stronger the building and the easier it goes up. Time spent on foundations pays dividends. Plants ordinarily require good root systems to flourish. Some have deep roots, some roots are broader based, depending on their circumstances. Buildings, plants and people come in all shapes and sizes with differing requirements. Their common aim is to be individually and collectively as effective as possible, and this calls for good foundations. Anything based on a careless approach to building will be high-maintenance and less likely to survive. Top-heavy construction is an accident waiting to happen, and life is no exception. The superficial accelerating style we now adopt towards living means our foundations usually lack sufficient substance to underpin our efforts and provide any sustained satisfaction.

Our minds play a big part in our happiness and healthy functioning. Learning how to best deal with them, rather than succumbing to their more than occasional trickery, is crucial. This intriguing art, that provides foundations for a much better life, could be called wisdom. Time now to visit a few places that contain an abundance of this precious commodity.

Calm

Proper foundations require adequate space, and likewise we need to clear our heads to accommodate supportive wisdom. Regrettably, the value of calm is seldom explained and few of us know how to access it.

Imagine trying to drive down a road full of traffic coming from all directions, and you have a picture of what our minds are continually subjected to. In fact, near constant mind activity is our modern norm. (Seemingly we each have more than fifty thousand thoughts a day.) When our energy isn't devoured by ceaseless thinking it can be channelled elsewhere gainfully. Reduced mental noise allows us to be more aware, and less at the mercy of impulsive behaviour. Our minds are like a glass of water, if we stop throwing things in they settle, enabling creative ideas and solutions to emerge.

Learning to clear our heads is a gradual process of expanding benefits and there are many well-established effective methods. Calming techniques have been taught for thousands of years. We might be forced into them by a serious upset, or approach inquisitively. Natural activities like physical work, walking and doing chores (particularly outdoors), help to release tension. Talking and crying, when appropriate, provide emotional outlets. Simple procedures like finger tapping points of the body can also have a considerable calming effect. (I have known this to relieve anxiety within minutes.) Meditation, baths, and soft music all enable us to wind-down. Touch can help too. This could be holding hands, hugging, massage, stroking animals, touching plants or even materials.

Touch and proximity are potent human comfort tools we often neglect. Certainly there are boundaries to be respected, within which touch and closeness provide substantial support and relief. Tests show fear stress is reduced by holding the hand of a stranger, and further reduced by holding the hand of a spouse. Family and friends hug to greet, celebrate and reassure. Monkeys use mutual grooming as a means to build trust and rapport, just as we normally enjoy having our hair stroked or bodies massaged. We can also be 'primed' to like strangers by merely holding hot drinks (this may be because touching warmth reminds us of the womb).

Eventually the idea is to be content spending time alone with our thoughts, watching them and our reactions while taking in what's around without additional stimulation. Attempting this is where we meet ourselves for the first time and are shocked by the extent of our restlessness. (Observing the places our thoughts drag us to can be quite amusing.) We realise we are a long way from being at ease. Directing attention into our breathing and various parts of the body can help. With a little practice, advice and willpower this gets easier. Listening to silence and the sounds that pass by generates enriching new experiences. We learn to relish simpler, quieter time away from the fuss of a busy mind exacerbated by others in the same boat.

Admittedly, trying to separate ourselves from the noise our agitated minds create is testing at first. Initially it produces feelings of boredom, loneliness or worry, urging us to resume responding to the incessant demands for stimulation our heads are accustomed to. As we get over the cold turkey of being without people, noise and distracting stuff for a while, things settle to what is probably our more natural state, or pace, of mind. We calm down and begin to see, feel, hear, smell and savour what we have rarely encountered. A warmth flows in and our sensitivity changes. Gradually it makes our thinking more coherent, as sleep does. Surprising emotions can rise to the surface, followed by peaceful feelings which intrigue us to dwell for a time or go further into an Aladdin's Cave of treasure. We are unearthing something in us that feels deeply connected and it has an intoxicating draw. As we unwind, revisit and explore, who knows where this might lead?

Don't underestimate the returns of this process. Watching our thoughts calmly and silently till they subside is a vibrant type of consciousness heralding progressively illuminating perspectives.

The remarkable thing is, how difficult such an apparently straightforward undertaking like being alone with our thoughts turns out to be. When we experience the benefits it is hard to believe how, what is ostensibly, doing nothing can feel so good and improve our overall functioning so much. Initially it takes a bit of work (they say the first twenty minutes are the longest) but it's well worth a proper try. It could be the most significant tool you ever pick up.

Psychology

We have opinions, expectations, hopes and fears that continually flow through our minds. Where do they come from and are they helping or hindering us? Thoughts and beliefs determine much of our behaviour, and Psychology could be called the science of behaviour. Psychology is generally regarded as a discipline to address specialist issues, whereas it's most profitable use may be in figuring out how *we* tick and where it stems from. Admittedly analysis *can* lead to paralysis, Psychology certainly does have it's overindulgences and limitations. Still, it is a very handy instrument in the liberating voyage of self-discovery if we adopt a pragmatic approach.

It's worth recognising that many Psychological illnesses are linked to FEAR. Extreme manifestations can be complex disorders with severe symptoms requiring specialist attention.

As a routine treatment, Psychology often deals with containment or the symptoms of problems rather than root causes. The likelihood of this is increased when Psychologists are constrained by the remit of their Health Authorities, which is common. Similarly, useful Psychology-based spin-off techniques don't dig deep for answers, yet they can appear impressive in some contexts.

Revealing

Personality profiling based on consistent correlations is widely accepted. There is no magic to this, so it looks like we are more readable than we realise. Everyone *is* unique, nevertheless our traits can be categorised to show how we will usually react to various circumstances. Suitability for jobs and what we tend to be attracted to or put-off by in people, are also fairly predictable. The precise details that determine our personality formation may be awkward to pin down, the way we turn out is less of a mystery. Many elementary tests exist that divulge readily applicable personal temperament hints. These give us a head start in life and their disarming accuracy can stimulate an advantageous curiosity.

Damage Limitation

Most of us try to avoid certain emotions without really recognising the manoeuvres involved. This not only restricts our life but also prevents detection and treatment of weaknesses. So we hobble around, emotionally impaired, looking for something familiar we can rely on not to expose our fragility. This is the convoluted cover-up many of our lives have turned into, and any attempt to unmask it is typically met with considerable apprehension or hostility.

If acute emotional pain surfaces and persists, we might be forced to seek some relief from Psychology. Time moves on and the worst may pass without us necessarily detecting the true source. In such cases it is normally just a matter of time before another difficulty causes the misery to return, quite conceivably in another guise.

Significantly, a new wound on top of an old wound aggravates the injury, compounds the pain, and leaves us prone to further damage. This vicious cycle applies emotionally as well as physically. If we locate the real source of weakness, it can be treated and steps then taken to reduce future harm.

Old wounds are not our only snag. Learned behaviour, used in childhood to obtain relief, often creates more complications in adulthood than it solves. The well-worn assumptions that lie behind entrenched behaviour make us take it for granted. Counterproductive tactics go unnoticed, as they continue to sabotage our happiness and freedom. Clues lie in recurring emotional setbacks, which may eventually force us to consider that *we* could also be part of the cause, not just the common denominator. Thorough careful digging to expose the roots in our past can reveal detrimental, often transferred, fixed mindsets. Exploring this, with or without specialists, can yield means for future improvements. These enable us to act prudently when overly taxing emotions relate to sources in ourselves, rather than focusing solely on the symptoms or external triggers. Then we are liable to experience less emotional discomfort, disruption and confusion. However, regardless of what we discover, our conditioning remains an issue albeit perhaps diminished.

One way or another we all acquire a load of emotional baggage, views and approaches, many of which are then carried throughout life unnecessarily. They weigh us down and contribute to repeated troubles. If only we would spot these burdens and learn how to drop them when required, how much lighter living could be. We can access Psychology to facilitate this before things go really sour, or we can wait till life makes us an offer that can't be refused, as most folk do.

It Makes Sense

The widespread frustration and associated obsessiveness of everyday life aren't considered dysfunctions yet or we might all be Psychology patients, and there wouldn't be enough Psychologists to treat the Psychologists, never mind the rest of us. In any case, raising personal awareness of our emotional make-up by whatever means can contribute to a better climate for progress, less self-inflicted hardships or restrictions, and more relevant lifestyles.

Relief

There is a wealth of useful approaches to ease emotional suffering. Time plays a big part as we all know, and often forget in the eye of a storm. Talking and writing down our thoughts can aid clarity and afford some relief. Crucially, improvement is more likely when we admit to being lost or confused and are prepared to 'put everything on the table'. Otherwise we can spend a lot of time trying to avoid our more fundamental issues, making the search for real progress a wasteful charade. A 'child' remains in all of us, asking to be heard in times of intense emotional pain. We would do well to listen and console this vulnerable voice from the past instead of ignoring it's needs and concerns, thus adding to our pernicious despair.

Regularly when our ego takes a knock we frantically endeavour to deny the experience using various methods. These include – striking out, burying the effects, a change of emphasis, a simple transfer of our usual behaviour to more amenable subjects, or whatever combination of tactics offers us the desired reassurance. It can be problematic but we usually get there, which is back where we started ready to recreate another version of our drama sooner or later. (Some say depression is the ultimate lie detector. It may be our mind's way of telling us to stop and try another way, but that doesn't mean we take heed.)

Occasionally we really *have* had enough. The distress could be too great to gloss over, our transfer options could be limited, or we may have seen versions of the same 'scary movie' too many times before to ignore the possibility that we might have had a hand in its making, along with being the main character. Like a crumbling dam, our resistance has been pushed beyond it's limits. We are weary and forced to allow what is happening to come out, unrestricted. Emotionally we may have reached one of the lowest points in our life. Sadly, it can take this level of desperation for us to open new doors. (Actually they are very old doors, just new to us.) After a big knock some of us stumble upon them, and that's how *I* learned.

Following several weeks of feeling very low, I finally said to myself one morning, 'This isn't a life, this is no way to live.' I didn't comprehend I had been trying desperately to avoid my situation rather than facing up to it. I was losing my battle against the full force of reality and couldn't continue the fight. You might say I was now surrendering. Within an hour my desperation lifted and never returned. I had a long way to go but the worst was over. If only I had realised my habitual attempts at avoidance had actually been making matters worse. Coping mechanisms I acquired to deal with my more painful emotions in childhood had taught me to stifle hurt feelings where possible or cover them with toughness. This shaped my entire life. It was so automatic, I didn't appreciate what was taking place. No one told me I couldn't grow and start living properly until I allowed my full range of emotions to be felt, which by now was within my coping limits. One of the main reasons I'm writing this is to help others by explaining what I had to learn the hard way; what I almost never learned. Surrender and learn. Allow feelings to have their full say; recognise the compounding associations from childhood where possible; then the deep healing begins. This facility has presumably been built into our design over thousands of years to deal with the harsh realities living brings. It may be what the grieving process is about – enabling us to soldier on and gradually recover, bruised but better equipped.

> *One day when a hunter returned to his cave he found it full of demons. He did all he could to remove them. He chased them, threatened them and pleaded with them till they were all gone. All except the largest and fiercest, which defiantly remained. Exhausted and resigned to his fate, the hunter placed his head in the mouth of the last demon... and it instantly disappeared.*

The transformation we can undergo from 'surrender' has been described throughout history in glowing terms by Religion in particular. We could say it's partly the surrender of self-will to greater forces, which is as much an acknowledgement of our limits as anything. Crediting Divine intervention that leads to wondrous all-seeing vision is a decidedly glorified explanation, although the relief involved makes these assertions understandable.

We are only prevented from using emotional surrender to obtain the prize of transcending tense existences, by contrived fears and unawareness of what we are supposed to be – fully functioning adults. There is no contradiction here between surrender on one hand and growing up on the other. Acknowledging our changing limitations is a key part of wisdom and growing up. It can take a lot of bravery (or despair) to face this but the enormous dividends far outweigh any demands. When you experience it many things fall into place, that's all I will say here.

The Duke Of Wellington was an acclaimed General. When asked what single attribute was paramount in a successful military leader, he is reported to have said – 'Knowing when to retreat.'

So, 'Groundhog Day' is ok for a while. Maybe even fun at times until the constant repetition, struggle and then pain turns into a living nightmare for even the most insecure control junkies. The impetus required to break out mainly comes from an exhaustion of all other possibilities. Those lucky enough to make it are not good or clever or gifted, they are just *ready*. Ready to face their toxic obsolete fears of emotional surrender and come up smiling. They have suffered enough at the hands of their self-imposed repression.

What takes place? No one completely understands the mysteries of human emotions. Conceivably we just get more in line with what is actually happening rather than pushing against it with our concocted versions, and so end up being carried easily in the ultimate flow of 'reality' where the greater power lies. Whatever is occurring, the main thing is we can feel a lot better, it can happen quickly, it can last and it can be built upon.

Growing up

Growing up is what we are meant to do and what we generally fail to achieve. Why? Because we don't have to in modern society. To make matters worse, we unwittingly spread our 'not growing up' attitudes at every opportunity.

Satisfactory adulthood involves many things which could be seen in part as – using our range of abilities sensibly with no entitlement expectations whatsoever. That is true liberation and it is very scary to mollycoddled children. I can hear you now. 'What? How can this be? I am important and special. My wishes must be met or I will get upset and complain or sulk.'

If our main approaches to life are complaining and expecting others to comply with our requirements, what have we become? Yes, spoiled children, that's what. We have lost contact with adult reality in our centrally heated, air conditioned, plumbed, powered and protected worlds. How did this happen?

...Because our water readily pours from taps. Our food lies on supermarket shelves just waiting to be collected at our convenience, or better still we can have it delivered to the door. Doctors attend to our health. Police attend to crime. Soldiers defend and fight for us. Employers pay us and provide benefits, in return for prescribed input. Labour-saving devices reduce our chores. Cars and other transport ferry us around. A world of opportunity, entertainment and social contact lies at our fingertips. Our living and working conditions are becoming increasingly 'comfortable' at an accelerating rate.

No wonder we feel entitled. By any historical standards, many of us do a whole lot less and get a whole lot more in return than ever before. Is this good? I think we could have a fair stab at the answer to that – yes and no. Sure we all want things to be better. We don't want starvation and disease wiping out our populations. Neither do we want to grow obsessive, neurotic, weak and ill from an excess of comfort and adverse lifestyles, as is now taking place.

As I mentioned previously, Mythology describes young adults being sent out on demanding endeavours to develop themselves. Their childhood notions were shattered by exposure to all kinds of extraordinary trials, journeys and demons. They emerged more capable individuals, worthy and appreciative of the challenges and rewards life had to offer. The concept is sound albeit somewhat embellished for effect. Resourcefulness is our key. Physical, mental and emotional resourcefulness is what gets us through and this requires tough lessons to be learned. There is no value in avoiding self-reliance, that only feeds insecurity.

How do we expect our children to walk, let alone run, if we won't allow them to stand on their own two feet? Yes allow. Not make or force; not even teach. This isn't cruelty. This is necessary natural programming we are suppressing. I saw a toddler walking down steps last week, refusing her father's hand. I clearly remember striving for similar independence at that age. Children don't want to stay dependent, it's suffocating. When will we learn to make a life for ourselves and encourage our children to find their own?

We can keep a bird caged and safe from danger, or we can set it free to live and learn; to take it's chances. Which do you think it would prefer?

Life is an opportunity, a challenge and a gamble, not a predictable entitlement – how dull that would be! We are dealt a hand, then improve our chances and those of our successors by playing the game and refining our skills as we play. Expecting others to play for us, or playing for others, is debilitating all round. We can't learn to live fully that way and we can't contribute or express ourselves sufficiently. Not using our abilities enough renders them rusty, leading to fears of losing or even trying which result in a reluctance to take potentially rewarding chances. So we remain unfulfilled spectators stripped of our prime function – the test of tackling life using our full range of capabilities.

The ups and downs are all part of a process that adequate exposure helps us to deal with.

We can unintentionally accelerate deterioration in old people by 'over assisting' them and reducing their input. Any life form deprived of it's full functioning will wilt, and it follows that people go progressively downhill where support is overly prescribed. This approach fosters an outlook which expects others to step in before we are encouraged to apply our own faculties to the full. A spiral of frustration and premature decline consumes the recipients in this enfeebling 'nannying' practice. What type of individuals and what type of species will emerge if we are not urged to take responsibility for bringing out the best in ourselves without reliance on, or expectations of, others?

Trust

If we want to reach a better understanding of how to live, considering our notions about reliability and trust ought to help. I'm not referring to contractual or working roles, duties and arrangements. This is about our 'should' demands and expectations of others.

As before, trust is not the fundamental issue. The issue is our customary self-centred interpretation of trust. What is trust? Is it expecting someone to do what we think or hope they should do, usually in our interest? Why should they do what we want them to do? This is the big question which exposes our delusions and selfish demands.

If we don't learn to look after ourselves we won't be much use to anyone. Yet, sometimes we expect others to ignore this glaring priority and favour what *we* deem acceptable. Granted, common interest makes fine sense to the fortunate enlightened few but what selective reasoning routinely expects others to place *our* requirements above theirs? Do we even consider they may have a unique changing personal agenda? What about specific circumstances that can have surprising effects on anyone's actions, including ours – do we take these into account?

The naivety of our expectations is highlighted by recognising what lies behind our *own* behaviour. Superficially we can appear altruistic at times, until we work out our self-interest takes many forms. We make sacrifices to avoid feeling bad; we give to feel good or receive in return; and we share to be part of something or avoid penalties. Most of us do likewise. Our actions tend to reflect our own best interests, despite what may appear to be the case. Accolades and awards for commendable generosity, while often valid, usually fail to take any underlying personal motivations into account.

Doing what is best for us is reasonable; expecting people

to put what is best for us ahead of themselves is childish nonsense. It makes living unnecessarily complex as we subject ourselves to the whims of others, hoping they will comply with our wishes and suffering when they don't. Give this up and life improves. Trust is a personalised idea that *we* choose to count on; we can only try to do so wisely and learn from the consequences. Like life, trust has few guarantees.

Be realistic. Everyone (including ourselves) does what is best for them, as they see it, at the time. Ok, now we're getting somewhere; now we're growing-up.

Love

A small word with a host of interpretations, most of which are inadequate. Significantly, I have chosen to include it here in the Found section rather than under Lost. Why, when we all know the distress love can cause, or do we? Many problems pose under the label of 'love' but on closer examination they are nothing of the sort. In fact, when love seems to be a headache we are often dealing with that old sheep in wolf's clothing – FEAR. Unintentionally confusing love with fear is one of the most painful and widespread traps caused by our failure to see the world as capable adults rather than dependent children. It doesn't help that we merely lift our ideas about love from the shelf of life that surrounds us, instead of using our reason to question these assumptions. If we did, perhaps all would be revealed. As they say, 'Seek and you will find.'

I confess love was a mystery to me for many years and I readily admitted this in my attempts to unearth any elusive significance it might possess. At least, even then, I knew something was missing. Reasonably happy relationships came and went with little mention of the word. It may have popped out impulsively on the odd occasion although there was never any lasting magic I could associate with love… until, I was ready.

Let's take a trip on the shifting seas of love, where we can explore the popular misconceptions that hinder and damage us. Who knows, if we're lucky we might find the key to pretty much everything that matters.

Before we proceed it's well worth bearing in mind that the word 'love' is purely a human label we are using to convey something. Feel free to use any word, or words, you prefer.

For our purposes we could say love has 3 levels of meaning. We'll start at the bottom and work our way up.

Lovetastic

We use the expression 'love' to show exaggerated liking or enjoyment. It is regularly accompanied by the word 'hate' as in, 'I love pies but hate bursting out of my jeans.' Not much to be gained here then.

Romancing

The most prevalent use of the term 'love' pertains to romantic relationships between two people. Our modern world is heavily influenced by the desire for this romantic love, and our lives can be shattered when it fails to materialise or comes undone. So is there something important we should know, and are we chasing phantoms?

YES!

If you want to head straight into a 'minefield' blindfolded, this could be the way. In fact, the greater our susceptibility to the romantic love experience, the farther we have strayed from our path and the less liable we are to find answers. (Conversely, persistent failure can supply the impetus for success when we refuse to settle for substitutes.) Am I saying we can't love or be loved? No, of course not. Is that a welcome sigh of relief I hear?

The pitfall of romantic love is not romance. Romance is wonderful, if perchance destined to wane. The rock we perish on is *wanting to be loved*. Irrespective of how strong this desire feels before, during or after a relationship, it is *not* an adult human need. There is a world of difference between wanting and needing.

The chances are, a strong desire to be loved in adulthood comes from a perception in childhood of being inadequately or inappropriately cared for. Early perceived failures frequently reveal their formidable hold when exposed or even touched upon in later life. Moreover, it's likely that intimacy in adult relationships taps into strong underlying mental connections created by the intimacy of our most formative years. These mighty undercurrents can all too easily carry us into wearying waters.

When our valid scepticism questions the strength of a hidden adult 'love' link to early childhood, we should consider the amount of childlike behaviour that surfaces in romantic relationships. Hand holding, cuddling, baby-talk, chasing, tickling, huffs, tantrums, mutual grooming and feeding all emerge. Then there is the curious 'coincidence' that virtually every love song ever written harks back to our earliest vocabulary and pleadings. 'Baby, baby, please don't go! Baby come back! Baby I love you! Daddy! Daddy! Momma!' We have heard them so many times and their consistent, infant-like, pleas are telling. They feasibly point straight through the current object of desire towards the parents of the writer, no matter how convoluted that route may be. (Kinda knocks the shine off all that luvvy duvvy stuff a bit, doesn't it.)

The pain of loss, or fear of potential loss, in close adult relationships can be compounded terribly by our childhood.

Without us knowing, the recent distress acts as a catalyst unlocking old dormant insecurities. When this happens, the hurt emotions can get very protracted and overpowering as we focus on the latest 'other party' rather than our childhood where the root causes probably lurk.

Romantic Radar

Outdated selection mechanisms add to the snags of romantic love. When we fail to recognise these, then proceed to overlay them with our romantic notions and childhood insecurities, we become embroiled in an almighty tangle.

What we find attractive or otherwise is partly derived from early experiences. Mismatching is a common consequence, and repeated relationship 'failures' indicate that our antennae are deceiving us. Applying compatibility associations from childhood is overly simplistic and often causes disappointment because we are now adults living in a very altered world that we have failed to reassess. It would be wise to learn the difference between our past, present and even future compatibility requirements, rather than jumping headlong into the romantic rapids at the slightest hint of attraction. Unfortunately, this pivotal precaution rarely reaches the top of our priority list.

Romantic Realities

There is another side to romantic love. Nature is smart, very smart, sometimes too smart for us. It shrewdly employs compelling impulses, focus and inducements to facilitate our procreation. As far as Nature is concerned, what we call 'romantic love' has a cardinal motivation that fuels it's potent allure – reproduction.

Essentially we are being expertly lured for purposes that may not be entirely beneficial to us as individuals. Nonetheless, any trace of surface attraction, with the possibility of some pleasure or feeling wanted, is often enough for us to eagerly succumb regardless of the risks or complications we face.

Mythology, Religion and History all warn about the dangers of playing with strong natural drives but we seldom take heed. We are continually caught-out by limited romantic ideas about love, and our arrested development makes us super-easy prey nowadays. We expect to take what we want, in a sort of popularised 'smash and grab' on Nature, without realising there is more to the story and our contribution. The bigger picture isn't just unclear to us, it's a complete mystery. By separating the pleasure element (what we take) from it's proper complement (what we offer), we think we have won. That is until we are forced to learn tough lessons, usually delivered from the painful ramifications of our patchy appreciation. No surprise then how love stuff invariably falls short of it's enormous hype, when we don't play our full part or don't want to.

There are a number of ways to describe our underlying premise behind romantic love. 'Taking more than giving' or 'conditional love' both cover it reasonably. In this standard 'love' formula, any thought of the other person's best interests must ultimately remain subservient to our own, especially when the meeting of our apparent needs comes under threat. Sure, we may look after, fuss over and compromise with our partners; though we normally have one overriding motive – our personal 'requirements'. There is little love here, mainly fear. Just listen as we demand others place us at the top of their consideration list. If this isn't childish fear at work, I don't know what is.

Romantic Residue

To sum up then; the indications are – feeling loved is a childhood survival and development need which retains considerable control over adults. It combines with Nature's pervasive priority to reproduce, and surfaces in the guise of 'romantic love' with all it's transient thrills and related insecurities. The dependency that ensues inhibits our personal growth and contributes to relationship 'breakdowns' for all but the fortunate few, and the most insecure of us who cling desperately to anything that avoids loss or self-reliance. Lucky winners are rare here and what we choose to do about it may affect the substance of our entire lives.

Doesn't sound like there is much hope for love then?

…Except for the remaining love we have yet to investigate. Thankfully, what *it* brings is exceptional.

Being Love

Assumptions about romantic love have blurred the picture and left most of us spinning. A few lucky folk may have learned about lasting love from balanced parenting or early life encounters though regrettably, modern emphases on selfish considerations make this increasingly unlikely, so we usually miss precious opportunities for greater happiness.

We are not bad or stupid here, just slightly lacking in vision. Maybe this will help...

I have an image in my mind of a mother lovingly feeding her baby. The baby grows up and lovingly feeds their own child. The taker has become the giver, and that to me is love in action with it's responsibilities, caring relationships and rewards. Unconditional giving and taking forms hugely gratifying, changing bonds. Most of us fail to fully savour these because we are too busy chasing our own 'needs', still being or wanting to be looked after by parents, a partner or society.

Childhood has provided lessons for our role as adults, not excuses to remain children. The past has gone and we no longer require what we did then. Searching for it (trying to take love) in adulthood is hopeless. If we give that up we ought to find answers. Adopting the parts we are suited to, applying the helpful lessons we learned as children, and giving what we benefited from or what we lacked previously, are important contributors to our optimum functioning. We either take these chances or continue to run in circles chasing a mirage. Encouragement, reassurance, assistance, guidance; that's what works, that's a big part of love. Many of adulthood's finest returns lie in appropriate giving, understanding, caring, sharing and loving. Appropriate is a key word here. Too much or misplaced care and giving can be harmful.

Recently millionaires volunteered to help and inspire disadvantaged people. Many of the givers emotionally admitted they had never felt so fulfilled. Besides money, they used their practical talents together with close personal input to empower less fortunate strangers. It wasn't just about giving. That's not love, that's charity. They got involved; tried to figure-out what was suitable; and carried things through. Both parties benefitted enormously from this mutual connection – a win:win for sure.

Love Story

A traveller and his dog came across a white palace with marble steps leading to huge golden doors. They ventured up the steps where the traveller cautiously knocked on the doors. A beautiful woman in long white robes answered. 'Can you tell us what this place is please?' asked the traveller politely. 'Yes, certainly,' said the woman in a soft voice. 'This is Heaven.' 'Oh,' said the traveller, 'We have searched many years for such a place and it looks truly remarkable, as I expected. Can I please come in?' 'Yes, of course,' replied the woman, 'But we don't accept dogs. You will have to leave yours outside.' The traveller paused for a moment then declined courteously. He would not leave his companion behind. So they both strolled down the steps to continue their journey… together.

A little further ahead, at the top of a green hill under a pale blue sky, the sun was shining on a peaceful well. An old man sat beside it drinking water. 'Do you mind if we take some water?' asked the traveller. 'We have been walking several hours.' 'Help yourself,' responded the old man with a warm smile. Sitting drinking next to them, the traveller couldn't help feel a certain comfort around this old man and the well, so he commented, 'This seems a pleasant spot, does it have a name?' 'Yes indeed,' replied the old man,

'This is Heaven.' 'Heaven!' gasped the traveller, 'But I thought we just passed Heaven?' 'Oh no,' said the old man knowingly, 'We put that there to tempt anyone who would abandon their friends.'

Love Barriers

Unless we experience fitting love in childhood, we run the risk of being confused and afraid about life and love – disconnected. Barriers arise to protect us from our confusion, hurt and fears. The complication with these unacknowledged barriers is that – they may have reduced the damage of painful feelings when we were children, but they became obstacles to valuable expression and connection in adulthood. The tide turned but our walls stopped the waiting waters flowing as intended. We can spend our entire lives on autopilot feverishly maintaining barriers, attributable to childhood, that block connecting love. These all too common circumstances skew our emotions, even enabling us to focus on 'impressive achievements', without the achievers ever experiencing a completeness of being. We extend the error by admiring such achievers without considering their emotional sacrifices, questionable lifestyles and possible linked health issues. Continually struggling to achieve new goals or searching for what seems missing, points to emotional barriers, distortions and disconnections resisting the free flow of love with the contentment it instills.

When asked for the answer to life, a sage replied, 'Love.'
When asked what the impediment was, he said, 'Fear.'
When asked what it is we fear, he replied, 'Love.'

You could say an enveloping love, that often requires considerable digging or a trauma to reawaken, lies deep within us all. Maybe we are born with it but the world gets in our way. Think of a faint smouldering glow covered by charred embers that need prodding, fanning and something to burn on. When the fire catches it produces a vigorous flame, and that is one way to describe the love in us. Remove the barriers and it will take over. This 'love' is a word for what may belong at the centre of our lives, and when we restrict it from radiating through us we exist without being fully alive. When we are afraid to love we're afraid to live; and I expect you can't begin to fathom what on earth I'm rambling on about. That's alright, at least we're trying.

Love In Action

Without *any* love, our barriers and self-absorption would quite conceivably be the end of us. The truth is, a whole lotta love manages to filter through despite our oblivious meanderings...

Love is us at our best and it isn't always easy. It lets us give with no need of return. It allows us to receive goodwill without feeling obliged to others. It calls error for what it is without condemnation. It offers civility without tolerating abuse. It makes friends and families rush to aid or protect each other. It makes us give-up everything for a cause or a dream. It enables us to hold on when all seems lost. It allows us to let go for the sake of another when we don't want to. It shows us how the best things in life are free. It demands of us when we see suffering. It forces us to hold back and let someone learn when it would be quicker to assist. It teaches us to be fair with others and tells us to be easier on ourselves. It shows us the value of our positive influence. It grieves while appreciating life's fragility and uncertainty. It makes grown men cry like babies with relief or thanks or joy when they see selfless kindness. And it makes people lay down their lives without hesitation if necessary, for strangers they have never known.

Although love is painful on occasions, without it we are surely incomplete.

In the short burst dash for euphoria, romantic love wins hands down until the drug wears off. Then, among the debris and throughout life, there lies the seeds of a lasting, widespread, positive love that can take us much further. It appears frequently in various unassuming everyday guises we fail to spot. The enormity of it's power is constrained by our emotional barriers, or attentions being fixed on self-interest. Nevertheless, it has provided a vibrant illuminating force throughout history for many (often only after they were willing to look more carefully than before and change tack).

I got lucky by dropping my resistance, and love rushed through the gaps I allowed to open.

Love And Me

After years dismissing love, it got *to* me. You could say I finally understood the concept of unconditional love, or saw how conditional my interpretation of love had been, and why.

This is no charity giving, be nice to everyone, goody goody, syrupy, gushy, flag waving evangelism we're discussing. (I'm not saying charity or being nice is a bad thing, it's not.) I'm alluding to something much more intrinsic, comprehensive and satisfying.

My story is that one day a friend said, 'You can tell there is a lot of love in you.' That was it. Sounds straightforward, and it was. This unexpected description of myself was a notion I had never considered but, due to a recent emotional tumble, I was more open to new ideas than before. I wasn't renowned for my readiness to contemplate the views of others towards me, let alone accept them. In fact, prior to my latest setback, I thought I knew everything worth knowing about me, or anything.

My raw disappointment, combined with the intriguing new 'love in me' concept, led to a more studious look in the mirror. Did I have 'love in me' that I was hiding or denying to my detriment? Then I remembered times in the past when my readiness to aid strangers was so impulsive it raised eyebrows among friends. I felt helping was the right thing to do and I enjoyed it. Was this symptomatic of a dormant connection?

Furthermore, I couldn't recall much empathy towards me when I was young. Did those early impressions produce a lifelong compensating confidence act that had fooled myself more than anyone? Maybe I never learned much about kindness or caring, and maybe it was desperately banging to be released rather than squeezed to bursting point in a detached, well-rehearsed, confidence act. Should I admit to emotional confusion? That was a real test, but a curiously liberating one after so many years of 'managing' my feelings. A change beaconed; a disconcerting openness if you like; a total turnaround in many ways. Why was it so uncomfortable, and was discomfort the clue to a depriving history of repression?

There was another force working on me at the time. What if I applied this new open, unconditional mindset towards strangers? Rather than doubting from the outset, give them the benefit of the doubt. After all, we are just wary children in adult bodies trying to cover it up and do our best (I learned that later). There appeared to be an untapped power in this approach. A poker face comes across as threatening and reinforces barriers whereas an affable disposition reassures people and encourages them to be more at ease. They say you make the world you live in and I was beginning to see how. The more I thought about it, the more I realised I had been making life hard for myself, and that the reasons for my attitudes lay firmly in the past. They might never leave but their negative effects could be curbed. Thankfully I made the conscious decision, in the face of certain humiliation, to really give this 'new love' a try. The cost would be high, the benefits potentially immeasurable.

This internal dialogue took no more than a few minutes and that was it. Eureka! Everything changed. So much more made sense and I felt a weight had been lifted from my shoulders. I think I stopped resisting something that readily flowed from my willingness to consider this – lots of love in me, and everyone else, concept adequately. More significantly, what I would describe as a deep warm glow (that surely couldn't last?) ran through me. I remember being pleasantly surprised it was still around after ten minutes. This happened years ago and, despite becoming partly accustomed to the feeling, I can't appear to shake it. Suppose I just have to put up with that. Everyday things like plants, animals, people, the sky and the smell of the air are so much more invigorating, more sort of alive. It's as if I've tuned in to fascinating yet basic feelings. I can only surmise that whatever barriers I had put in place to protect me long ago had reduced, and something fundamental was now circulating as intended. You could call it love.

The big improvement or freedom is possibly that – giving love, or letting it flow, doesn't require much from anyone else whereas being loved obviously does. Reliance on others is bound to leave us more vulnerable, anxious and needy, no matter how capably we manage to hide it.

Anyway, from never crying, I began to shed a tear at lots of stuff like suffering, compassion and other people's joy. Sounds very strange I know and it was all new to me. Additionally, my tedious talent for acquiring colds every six months has since dissipated. I have been colds and sore throat free for several years. (The last occurrence immediately followed an argument, providing insight that I may be fairly able to deal with stress but it is also able to deal with me, quite firmly.) I've calmed down, and various forms of calming have been the cornerstone of many therapies for centuries. Who knows what broader health benefits I'm also deriving? Time will tell. My world continues to settle and open up. Chasing old rainbows is a thing of the past, while my growing interest in exploring life leads me to places and topics I previously dismissed or never thought to consider. I've also acquired a new ability (or uncovered an old one) to improve the outlook of others. I enjoy this and hope to use it much more very soon. This book is a big part of that, and once my sojourn with the necessarily solitary task of writing is complete, it will be full (or moderate) steam ahead wherever my fresh enthusiasm takes me.

FIND A BETTER LIFE

The Road To Love

Most of my appetite for improved awareness came after a torrid emotional episode forced me to reassess, and that is common. I may never have learned much of any lasting value without a few kind words from a friend at a time when I was ready to see myself differently – thanks a million Mary! Unearthing what I have discovered requires a fortuitous mix of circumstances, not altogether pleasant. They say we have to suffer to grow. On the other hand, I didn't have this book to help me (although there were assorted sources that did). I just hope my experience and thoughts will prove useful in *your* search for better ways.

The 'A ha!' of love is an ideal place to start. The escalating advantages of breakthrough and freedom follow steadily.

Action

Irrespective of how appealing it sounds, we can't just sit around all day wallowing in a new found glow of love hoping for the best. So what *should* we do, what should we avoid and when? There's no easy answer to that. Across the board recommendations are crude devices –

'One man's meat is another man's poison.'

Everyone is unique; every situation is unique; and everything is in a constant state of flux, however subtle.

If you think I can tell anyone the best way to live, think again. I can't. No one can. That's what we learn. Sure, advice is available and useful at times but if we need to be told how to live we stay lost and dependent.

It can be very complicated, or very simple and obvious. No one knows all the answers and the sooner we get to work finding our own, the better. That's life and that's what makes it interesting.

Types of action may be predominantly good for us or bad for us, which is where the value in established advice ordinarily lies – our welfare. Nonetheless, good/bad or right/wrong simplifications are how we teach children. There is a lot more to take in beyond that. After a while we have to learn about nuances, uncertainty, actions and consequences, and stop relying on others or we fail to blossom.

A young man lost his horse. When he told his father how awful this was, his father replied, 'Maybe.' The horse returned a few days later with several other horses. When the son told his father how fortunate this was, his father replied, 'Maybe.' A few days later the son fell from his horse, breaking a leg. This time he asked his father if it was as serious a setback as it appeared (the son was learning). His father predictably replied, 'Maybe.' Next week, the Emperor's army came to the village taking every able-bodied young man to fight in the war. The son was left at home due to his broken leg.

Regardless of first impressions we can experience unforeseeable twists in the tale, and as we know from smarty pants Chaos Theory – minor variations can lead to massive differences in outcomes. Robert Burns aptly pointed out…

'The best laid schemes o' mice an' men, gang aft agley.'
(Our most careful plans can stray well off course).

Getting Going

We may acquire abundant tools for life, establishing how and when to use them is the next step. Fixed ideas leave us straightjacketed, experimenting and learning should never end.

Think of a cocktail or a garden or a recipe. We adjust them to suit our varying tastes and the ingredients available. That is living. Using what is appropriate and appealing; trying different things from time to time and building a bigger picture, a suite of tastes and options. Moving at a suitable pace; altering it where necessary and when possible. Going further; looking closer; taking a step back; trying a new route; not rushing; not just copying or following. Now we're cookin'; now we're learning; now we're growing; now we're living. Where are we going? Nobody knows. That's not the crucial point. It's being on the adventure, we have been forged over innumerable years to tackle, that invigorates us. Pretty soon the cobwebs vanish and we wonder why on earth we bothered about all the nonsense. Now there is so much more to discover and enjoy. If you think you're past it or not ready, you're probably making excuses that prolong missing out.

Age, gender, aptitudes, moods, health, experience, knowledge and a host of other factors affect what we do and how. They interact, they change and they don't always apply, or apply in the same ways or to the same extent.

Try asking, reading, thinking or just jumping right in if it's not too deep. Making 'mistakes' is another way to learn. We soon find out what works or doesn't. You can ponder but not forever – reading the menu to separate what appeals from what doesn't is fine; eventually we have to choose or starve to death deliberating.

Setbacks can prompt us…

For years I depended on my good friend's availability to go out at weekends. One night he called off at the last minute, and this latest disappointment finally made me go it alone. Apprehensively I wandered into town, determined to try another way, and never looked back. It may not have been the most eventful evening of my life but it was one of the most liberating. I had broken my self-imposed chains, and from then on regularly ventured out unaccompanied. I met new people in new places and no longer relied on anyone in particular to socialise. It took a few more years and some bravery to savour the benefits of similar independence on holidays, day trips, eating out and more. The world is changing. Increasingly we can mix with others without relying on them, and benefit from fresh exploits, if we use our courage, initiative and determination sensibly.

Different Angles

There are a variety of views on any topic. (That's worth bearing in mind). Impulsiveness sparks rash choices; over-deliberating leads to missed opportunities. Waiting to rescue could mean someone drowns; jumping in without due consideration could mean everyone drowns. A little knowledge is dangerous, and too much can lead to inertia. Compromising might work, or bog us down. Take pacifism, it's a noble aim but a bully's dream invitation. Celibacy teaches us restraint, that could destroy our species in a hundred years if we all adhered to it. The downside of 'virtue' can be too much sacrifice and failure to live a full life. The saint has his shortcomings; the sinner is in every one of us and isn't *all* bad.

Dangerous snakes, insects and wild animals contribute to our diverse world. Care is definitely required around them, teaching us to be alert. Exposure to viruses is what drives our immune systems to improve, or a common cold would kill us. We don't like being sick but our body tells us when we have had enough and forces us to rest for our own good.

We think murder, disease and personal loss are terrible things. They are. The fact is though, they happen and therefore challenge us to deal with them and learn. When we do, coping and prevention are more likely. Failure, disappointment and upset all teach us how to cope. Avoiding them at all costs is avoiding life, and when they inevitably *do* catch up with us the pain is intensified by our underdeveloped coping skills. Calm down, I'm not saying, 'Aim to suffer.' I'm saying a bit of suffering is to be expected and necessary.

We mainly don't want to fight although sometimes we must to escape being swept aside callously. Fighting or fighting by another name is everywhere and it isn't only human physical battles that are being sorted out. Feuding intellectual philosophies and doctrines, personal emotional tussles and widespread petty point-scoring permeate our cultures. In the rest of Nature – erosion, floods, earthquakes, volcanic eruptions, collisions, plants and animals all contain vying forces. Physical fighting provides a last resort in our case. It is certainly misused at times and can have severe downsides. That said, it has protected many lives and freedoms when employed appropriately… whatever that means? Complacency, or failure to acknowledge the threats countered by a preparedness to fight for what we believe, is both naive and very risky in the real world. Preparedness for defence, and strategic attacks, tap into potent natural mechanisms that can be beneficial if handled with care.

Although far from ideal, the threat of war reflects how we are for now. It serves as a formidable deterrent and an inducement to cooperate towards a climate of order, if not quite harmony.

Most things have their place. Our task is to acquire and continuously refine a range of approaches to deal with situations satisfactorily and reasonably.

Balance

Yin and yang. Chemical formulae; mathematical equations; the balance of Nature. Drug dosage. Boom and bust. Too many or too few. Too little then too much. Is anything more integral than balance? Is everything in some sort of natural equilibrium that means, when it slips, recovery is mandatory? I've heard it said all elements are 'aiming to become' iron as it is the most stable. Do our endeavours amount to nothing more than complying with an overall balance imperative, and experiencing the consequences of imbalance in order to stabilise? Maybe some universal equilibrium is a complex version of how our brains and bodies operate – many separate interdependent functions. Whatever is in play, all we can really do is attempt to improve our understanding of balance, making adjustments or letting it flow as we see fit.

Overreaction

Behaviour is one of many aspects which seem to reflect our balance criteria – occasional situations require extremes while most usually benefit from a more moderate approach (as our health probably does). Worryingly, a recurring tendency to swing from one extreme to the other within our individual or group range is commonplace. For example, standard work/play lifestyles can turn into struggle/party for numerous folk, finally moving towards depression/mania in severe cases. (Many of our so called 'great achievers' have been subject to extreme mood swings.)

Psychology suggests that our 'Adult' personality aspects sit centrally, helping to *balance* our 'Parent' at one end and 'Child' at the other. Without enough balancing 'Adult' we swing more markedly between our 'Parent and Child'. This trait is apparent in the bully/coward swing and counter-swing employed by many of us unconsciously. From the school playground to more mature relationships, and even in the most routine jobs, we can be seen seizing opportunities to impose our 'authority' on others, as compensation for our feelings of inadequacy carried over from times when we were on the receiving end of some type of 'bullying' (however contrived or disguised it may have been). Our widespread hierarchies, like boss/subordinate relationships, provide ample scope to dented egos seeking redress for subtle, or not so subtle, forms of 'bullying'.

Overrun

Exercise can provide a worthwhile energy outlet or do more harm than good.

Humans are built to exert themselves periodically – mostly for 'fight or flight'. Likewise, you won't observe many big animal species whose adults spend a lot of time running around apart from sporadic chasing or fleeing. Obsessive behaviour is rife in modern humans and as a result, many of us now tend to push ourselves too hard. We might have 'something to prove', or a fear of ageing, or we just copy what looks like healthy behaviour without questioning it.

Frequent running, especially on very hard surfaces like roads and pavements, contributes to serious joint injury caused by continually exceeding our impact absorption thresholds. In addition, exertion increases mental stress by triggering the 'fight or flight' responses necessary for any activity which drives our bodies harder. Regular exercise also produces an addictive chemical high, perhaps making it feel more favourable than it is. Therefore exercise calls for a carefully balanced approach.

Overdrive

People were around for thousands of years B.C. – Before Cars. Throughout the vast majority of that time, I expect we moved at a fairly regular pace and became accustomed to it. Accordingly, our physical and mental aptitudes would no doubt have been finely tuned to the speed and nature of our movements.

Boats, the wheel, horses, cycles and trains steadily changed the way we moved around. Lately we have accelerated exponentially using *faster* boats, trains, planes, spacecraft, and most commonly – cars. As we accelerate, our senses must process information more rapidly and this is demanding. These demands are met at a cost because, in evolutionary terms, we have not had sufficient time to adapt to a consistently increased pace. (I'm not the only kid who ever tried to run before he could walk.)

Cars deserve a special mention because they have changed much more than the speed we move around. Few examples better illustrate the scale of damage being inflicted by our lack of attention to prime factors that *drive* imbalanced lifestyles.

Cars have allowed us to work further from home, which seems handy until we learn the importance of 'close' communities to our welfare. Cars keep us warm in winter, cool in summer and dry in the rain, which seems helpful until we discover that our bodies require adequate exposure to a range of weather conditions if we are to maximise our natural adapting mechanisms and avoid becoming helplessly fragile. Cars move us around, which seems fine until we realise we have become lazy and unfit as a result – we drive to the gym for exercise and can't park close enough. If we left the car at home and walked or ran to the gym, we could benefit from being outdoors and need a lot less time in the gym. Cars give us our own space, which seems pretty desirable until we notice this contributes to an anti-social disconnection that can breed resentment towards others. Cars provide many jobs, which seems beneficial until we spot that these jobs often require stifling robotic repetition. Some people like car noises or to play and show-off using cars, which seems ok until we recognise that this is often another symptom of a failure to grow up and embrace adult attitudes sufficiently.

The number of cars on the road makes parking difficult and driving stressful. If you're unfortunate enough to have an accident in a car at speed, you will learn tough lessons about the price of accelerated progress. Cars are the fastest depreciating asset many of us will ever own, and a squanderous drain on our finances. The money we spend on traffic management, traffic policing, road building and road maintenance is astronomical. The insurance, maintenance, fuel and administration costs associated with cars doesn't bear thinking about. Their emissions pollute the air we breathe, and that is a considerable understatement worthy of serious scrutiny.

Don't get me wrong I'm no eco warrior. I accept cars can be useful. I like them. The trouble is, they are more of a liability than an asset in many respects.

Overpowering

B.C. could also stand for – Before Computers, our current ultimate 'tail wagging the dog' device. Human susceptibility to distraction and habit is highlighted by the attention our already saturated minds give to computers, as they drag us further into the tangle of narrow overstimulation and obsession. Spelling out the cumulative costs, laboriousness, dependency, withdrawal, physical and mental strain, and time 'wasting' involved with computers would require a book in it's own right. If you're interested, step back and think it through. They certainly speed up calculations, communication and information processing, but are their benefits proportionate to the time we spend on them and the toll they take on us?

Our contemporary emphasis is skewed by computers, creating a pricey imbalance for questionable returns. Hopefully this is merely a transient learning stage that will pass soon. Continuing improvements ought to render our time-consuming relationships, with any overly taxing generation of computers, obsolete in the not too distant future. We humans can then get back to being human, and leave mechanistic interacting to better suited, emotionless machines. This should be an important next step towards acquiring a more effective balance of priorities.

Nature

As we attempt to make the most of our lives, we have an ever-present teacher in Nature. Landscapes, plants, other creatures and natural events provide messages about our place and function in the mix. From them we can read a fair amount about what is likely to help us thrive or not.

Against the enormity of this backdrop that envelops us, our embellished daily dramas and fuss pale into insignificance and are exposed for the diversions they ordinarily create; whereas learning to pursue our development with an acceptance of some common thrust should help by putting us more in synch with Nature's central momentum.

Plant Life

The life cycle of plants, from seeds to fragile seedlings, growth, flowering, seed production and decay, demonstrates what life involves. Normally multiple seeds are produced for a few plants to survive. Young plants have different needs from established specimens. What works is passed from generation to generation and adapted along the way to improve their chances. Weakness, vulnerability and distorted habits are ruthlessly eliminated. A multitude of factors including soil, climate, congestion, predators, size, shape and appearance all influence success. Plants have defence and competitive workings as well as cooperative habits. Continuity usually depends on their flowers and fruit being attractive enough to encourage the essential participation of unsuspecting partners. Curiously, human life is more akin to these processes than most of us take time to digest.

Trees are sometimes used to illustrate connections within human life. People are like leaves joined by twigs and branches to the tree. Our connections and what we are connected to may be more fluctuating and less physically apparent but the strength of our emotional ties alone suggests we are not as separate as we appear. Like us, leaves, roots and branches are more linked to some than others. They develop in various forms to whatever extent can be supported, trying to find the best way for the sake of themselves and the tree. Soil and water feed the roots which support the tree. The tree supports the leaves which convert energy from the sun to feed the tree in return. It's a give/take/grow operation, reaching as far as it can in all directions. As time passes seeds are spread, fallen leaves provide nourishment for the soil, and the cycle continues. Disease or damage to any leaf, root or other part of the tree could prove expensive all round. Overall good health benefits every part although inevitably not every shoot succeeds.

Our human need for proper integrated foundations is comparable to the adequate root systems required to sustain healthy trees.

The dangers of 'wrapping children in cotton-wool' can be compared to the saplings we stake to provide early support. The props must be removed as soon as possible to prevent distortion and avoid restraining their growth.

Where we differ from trees and plants communicates as much guidance as our similarities, when we learn the language of awareness. Without digging too deep, it is apparent we are not rooted to the spot; we are not entirely reliant on the conditions of our location; and our inter-relationships appear to be more varied and significant. This suggests that – exploration, some habitat diversity, and flexible inter-personal associations are among the features our design favours.

The form of roots and branches can be seen throughout Nature, from internal body mechanisms to external processes such as streams flowing to rivers and then to seas. Am I implying everything is similar and connected in more ways than we imagine? I'll leave that for the moment. All I will say is, trees and plants have plenty to teach us.

Wild Life

If plants offer us lessons, other life forms provide advanced courses in enrichment. Animals, birds, fish, insects, bacteria and anything else that moves, more or less of its own accord, are our noble yet graciously oblivious tutors. (Perhaps I underestimate their cognisance?)

We consume Nature documentaries avidly, entertained by the habits, shapes and colours of wildlife. Like various other subjects, we fail to connect what we witness with our own lifestyles. So to bed then up in the morning and back to the grind, none the wiser. It's as if we regard human existence as merely an adjacent platform from which to observe Nature. How did we end up so isolated from much of what we are, and where is this taking us? 'Don't worry,' you say. 'We are caring more about Nature and our environment now. We also go walking, climbing and sailing. Surely we are learning?' Possibly, but I'm not convinced. What *truly* lies behind our efforts? Is it wisdom, or mainly frustration and anxiety creating obsessive behaviour. I would say that, in general, we remain lost with little grasp of what actually works for us and why. It's our primal nature with all the skills, drives and needs it entails that is continually overlooked. Sure we have become more civilised and sophisticated than animals thankfully, but underneath we are still what we were shaped over countless ages to be.

Our 'progress' owes much to harnessing animal design for our benefit, like the strong horse or the hunting wolf that gave us dogs. We 'break' their wild nature and breed it out to make them cooperate, failing to recognise this is exactly what has happened to us in modern society. We have been 'broken' as much as civilised in order to work obsessively in unnatural circumstances, leading to a watering-down of our all-round effectiveness. Lures of unnecessary comfort and compensation tempt us to sacrifice anything resembling a fulfilled life for a routine existence. Like pet animals we have turned into 'pet' people, with all the weakness and limitations that entails. No wonder many of us feel caged, frustrated and desperate for our next distraction. We are increasingly being asked to deny our nature, which is highly impractical if not eventually impossible. Like many creatures, we learn more adequately by exploring and dealing with situations using our personal faculties where practicable, not simply by following the directions of others. Authority and assistance can only be useful in moderation. By extending our reliance on prescribed approaches we reduce our judgement and creative skills. This produces less capable, incomplete individuals, more exposed to the drawbacks and dangers of insecurity, indecision and misguided action.

So, what can we learn from our 'less advanced' life forms that might remind and help us?

Where do I begin? Animal pack cooperation, *practical* learning, seasonal adaptation, attention to territories, endurance, relaxation and survival techniques are some of the many inherent capabilities humans also possess but fail to make the most of.

I hesitate to include the bonds forged between pets and their owners as testimony to the value of animals because it's a bit like proposing animals in a zoo are fun and interesting. The regular proximity of pets is mutually enhancing but animal life is more complete and demanding in the wild, thus that is where the relationships between our natural functioning and theirs are more profitably illustrated.

We can learn by observing how the distinct life stages of our closer animal relatives operate and fit together. The young play, watch and experiment in childhood to hone the skills they require to survive later. Parents and packs care for, chastise and train youngsters to be effective adults. From an early age, every one has to contribute by doing useful work. All participate in accordance with their place and aptitudes. They can't afford to sit around becoming less adaptable, self-absorbed and consequently depressed, as *our* societies often entail. Older generations remain active, passing on practical wisdom in ways we have left to a minority of niche 'knowledge' filtering sources. *Our* elders already lack purposeful activity and breadth of insight from succumbing to lifestyles that invoke apathy. Repetitive routines, a bit of socialising, a few trips or absorbing ever-more contrived and distant media messages is about as much as our restricted conditioning allows in the years ideally suited to imparting and building on lifelong wisdom.

Life Is Trying

I am struck by the way plants and wild animals rarely give up trying. All do what they must to achieve their aims. The doing is as vital to the cycle as the outcome. (Our 'advanced' ability to consider outcomes can lead to apprehension and inaction.) The spider will try, try and try again to spin that web. The prey will fight for life in the jaws of it's predator, and even escape on occasions. The sick have no medical care and soldier on. I reflect on the birds in my garden as the feeding sparrow defers to the magpie or the pigeon, who then allows the gull to take over as soon as it arrives staking it's claim. All are constantly under threat from next door's cat or a fox, if their vigilance lapses for a second. This is my back garden on the outskirts of a city, right in front of my nose, not the jungle. It's everywhere. They can show us a thing or two about the everyday need for good judgement skills and appropriate risks.

Self-protection, probing forward with care and measured risk taking are essential for the survival of most species. Success is enhanced by couples, groups, shoals, swarms and flocks combining to achieve a common goal that would be far outwith their individual capabilities. All are playing their part in Nature's shifting equilibrium.

Our ideas of good and bad or right and wrong seem to be contradicted or upheld by other species, depending on circumstances. Examining this paradox opens pathways that offer us an improved understanding of life's fluid and often harsh realities. Some birds have several chicks and peck most of them to death after a few days. Others have two or three chicks and the strongest ousts the weak from the nest to perish. Throughout natural history, the weak have been at the mercy of the strong and removed in ways we have come to find shocking. Looking beyond our valid compassion for a moment, it is evident this 'natural selection' has shaped our world by building strength and encouraging counter-abilities such as resourcefulness and cooperation. Thanks to this and other events, we now live in a world where brute strength doesn't necessarily prevail (although it does retain some advantages, as well as a powerful engrained illusion of advantage we have yet to overcome entirely).

Life Experience

Sheltered existences don't exactly equip us for the real world. For instance, if a lion tears Bambi's mum to pieces and devours her, it wouldn't make much sense to scream, 'Murder!' However, nowadays many of us would if we were exposed to this reality. Hunting and killing are aspects of life we find tough to witness, let alone participate in. (Raised in the city, I'm no exception.) In spite of this, we rear and butcher animals on an industrial scale to satisfy our appetites; a seemingly curious contradiction. As omnivores, our bodies benefit from meat; as a civilised species, questions arise concerning the justification of slaughtering. Then we run into the next snag. Our primal nature and food needs may enable most of us to accept wholesale killing of animals as long as it is carried out discretely and humanely, but by keeping this under wraps it ends up all the less palatable when brought to our attention.

The darker side of this is that an appetite for bloodthirsty 'sports' remains in several cultures, indicating we retain more primal urges than our apparent civilisation implies. It is necessary to avoid any judgement trap here if we are to acknowledge then deal with the situation. Humans demonstrate an array of behaviours from heartfelt compassion to extreme ruthlessness, and these have contributed to what you might call our current 'success'.

Restricting pertinent exposure or sweeping our urges under the carpet holds us back and creates complications. Cruelty and squeamishness are a few of the consequences. We are what we are and the sooner we face up to it the better. All creatures learn from carefully testing their instincts and dealing with the outcomes. Why can't we? I'm not advocating brutality and violence, absolutely not. Our task is to find or create conditions that use our instincts favourably. To this end, a closer Involvement with Nature should enrich us and help improve our attitudes to food chains, amongst other things.

We can nurture better-rounded thoughts and actions by participation in a mix of relevant experiences. As I said before, our inherent respect for the environment and fellow creatures is already reemerging in various guises. It should grow and strengthen if we provide suitable outlets for our natural mechanisms, rather than relying on patronising diktats and moralising fashioned from individual or collective anxieties that sometimes border on hysteria.

Life Is Shocking

Contrary to the impression our entertainment creates, most of life is pretty routine (which is partly why we enjoy staged drama and seek excitement). That said, change is always taking place even if the pace makes it barely noticeable most of the time... Until we are disturbed from our slumbers by the full force of Nature and taken aback. The lessons of life's unpredictability and our need to be alert have been delivered once again. If luck is on our side we will continue after the event, worse off and ordinarily not much wiser. The debris is swept up, casualties counted, preparedness questioned, then it usually slips out of our minds into the record books. We have a tendency to block out anything undesirable until it arrives rudely in our laps. This is often called denial, and it does have a couple of benefits. Firstly, we may have pressing demands which automatically override less immediate issues. Secondly, why dwell on remote likelihoods that ask us to continually reassess our priorities; we would never get anything done for worrying. Worry is debilitating, so we do what we can and cross our fingers. That is certainly the positive intention behind denial as a coping device however, modern humans seem to be masters at taking denial to another level.

We frequently prefer to abdicate responsibility and ignore warning signs until forced to do otherwise by extensive damage. Runaway financial systems focused on short-term gains and ego glorification, rife abuse and exploitation, political and religious dogmas leading to tragic conflicts, and housing people in Nature's known ticking time-bomb disaster areas are among the scenarios inclined to escape our notice until it's too late. We take a while to catch on, if at all. Are we more *re*active than *pro*active? Whatever the causes, closed-minded attitudes and paying lip-service to threatening possibilities appears to be our way so far.

We are highly exposed to Nature. At any moment our world could be destroyed by a collision from space or volcanoes erupting and blocking the sun for many years. There isn't much we can do about that for now, which leaves us to focus on what *can* be achieved by improving our cooperation and flexibility. It might be worthwhile turning our attention to a wider range of tasks where individual and overall interests are better served. Humans relish achieving goals irrespective of payment, and there are many of us ready and willing to be put to better use. Part of the difficulty is, this calls for strong wise leadership in a political process where point-scoring regularly overshadows the public interest; and *who* chooses the leaders? Us of course, with all our preconceptions and oversights. Don't be surprised then if we get caught out a few more times as we continue to chase the 'really important' stuff like – parties, prestige and prizes. Isn't that what we really want? Well, is it?

Climate change and other natural threats have always occurred. Our ancestors were very exposed to such hazards. They probably possessed well-attuned innate warning skills we have let slip. Another big difference was that people were likely to have been more adaptable in the past. If a flood arrived they moved, because they were less bound by mortgages, possessions and indoor lifestyles.

'Progress' has constrained us to adapting less in crucial areas.

Whatever the obstacles to devising more malleable societies, the work starts with our personal attitudes which help to shape the lives we live, not with Politicians or any other scapegoats. In a constantly changing world, physical or mental inflexibility is a hindrance. As Nature clearly demonstrates – life requires us to bend and flow with it's varying winds, tides and events.

Natural High

Being among Nature can be therapeutic because it takes us back to our roots... or does it? Well, it can. Escaping distractions for a while helps enormously in becoming grounded. The problem is, whatever we do with Nature is coloured by human influences, and therefore normally falls well short of it's potential.

Many of us go to Nature to protect or improve it, or to take on a challenge, and that is ok as far as it goes. Hunting and exploring, or modern watered-down versions of these primal interactions with the wild, do enrich us to a degree. Beyond this – being alone, taking our time, not applying human tags (like names or interpretations of plants, birds, animals or places) while absorbing raw Nature, uncovers welcoming associations. If we allow the saturating layers of conditioned thinking to subside, changes take place. In these circumstances Nature can stimulate, relax and enlighten in ways I can't describe. Try it. No, not describing, experiencing.

Spirituality

No this is not about contacting the dead, that's the domain of so called Spiritualists. Nor is it Religion, we've already covered that. Labels can be misleading, and few more so than Spirituality. In my view, if any subject delivers lasting benefits in some of the most important aspects of life, that subject is Spirituality. It's a fascinatingly relevant topic which could be labelled Happiness, Freedom, Peace or anything of that ilk.

As a child I was fed my fair share of Religion and it didn't add up to me. Spirituality supplies the foundations on which Religion is precariously perched, without the dubious claims that tax our more discerning scrutiny. So far no other insight has come close to making me feel as good as Spirituality does. If this sounds like a burst of preaching is on the way, it's not, that would be a contradiction in terms.

Spirituality has no shortage of stumbling blocks. In fact, it embraces some of the wildest notions and egos you will encounter. It panders to the disaffected and provides, not very well disguised, ruses for those seeking to circumvent reality. Ironically, these detours are depicted as paths to a *deeper* reality. My kind of Spirituality can't do that if it is to deliver. So, to enjoy the fruits of Spirituality, we must first remove some of the skin around it...

I would describe Spirituality as traditional wisdom concerning human functioning, refined through the ages. Unfortunately the refining is open to abuse and much misinterpretation. Remember, reading and writing was limited to a very few specialised individuals when these ideas were recorded. They employed one significant device to aid the less sophisticated majority – simplified complexity. If you have ever tried to learn anything from an expert or explain something intricate to a child, you will recognise this requirement. The understanding gap is so wide we can only use diluted versions, stories or metaphors. At best we are in 'a little knowledge is dangerous' territory. At worst the simplified version is taken to be actual, and when enough people jump to such conclusions things acquire various fixed meanings. This meant we usually passed-on variations of metaphors and stories, intended to expand our views, which came to be regarded as unquestionable truths. Imaginative creations were assumed to exist as opposed to being open concepts, thought up by ancient people for the purpose of teaching wisdom. We read about Masters, The Divine, Mystics, Enlightenment, and expect these to be other-worldly ultimate comprehension sources; destinations rather than human created stepping-stones to assist human searching. We miss the point, then argue about conflicting interpretations of missing the point.

Several contemporary Spirituality scholars have sought to validate *their* views by adopting pseudo-scientific terms such as energy, vibration and dimensions. Loose references to Quantum Theory are thrown in. They also rework classic themes of a mind that is more than our brain; a 'Big Mind' or 'Super-consciousness'. Tying-in other old concepts like past lives, an afterlife and Karma adds to the appeal while probably oversimplifying otherwise helpful topics for exploration. Maybe these theories have some validity but they are liable to be representations rather than prevailing realities. Notably, the child in us can be impressed by

'Teachers' of such bold beliefs, especially if we have a 'father figure' susceptibility.

Conspicuous by their absence in any Spirituality texts I have read, are references to the authors' relationships with their parents. This is important, if not pivotal, and could provide revealing indicators as to why they were drawn towards such a self-searching subject in the first place. It might go a long way to explaining their specific emphasis, outlook and conclusions.

Spirituality is not sacrosanct. We have to astutely assess and refine what we inherit if it is to be of continuing worth. To do this, once again we must be alert to the trap of surface impressions, and we have now covered much of that. So what *is* Spirituality saying, and how can it help?

Spirituality teaches us about ourselves and our place in the world. The importance of balance, calm, appropriate work and influences is emphasised. Love and clearer understanding lie at the core of many teachings, as do 'growing up' and flexible attitudes. Sounds familiar? That's right, this is a sort of modern Spirituality book (if you're in the business of labelling). These days Spirituality could also be termed Self-help, however the trouble with labels is that they only take us so far, and we're going further.

Early interpretations of modern discoveries in Psychology and Science can also be found in Spirituality, together with concepts we are still a long way from clarifying.

There are many remarkable Spirituality texts, and I fear I would spoil their meticulously crafted messages by attempting to convey too much here. If they teach us anything, they explain the need for personal searching and discovery, as in –

The student who never became a mathematician because he believed the answers at the back of his book. Strangely enough, the answers were correct.

Concise challenging stuff like that makes Spirituality a revelation and a treat. It contains copious amounts of humour and irony, enhancing it's appeal and realness. There are numerous rich sources on-line, in bookshops, libraries and religious scripture. Just be careful not to misinterpret them.

Loss & Found

I want to end this part of our voyage in what might seem unpleasant waters, on the surface.

Death is a situation we living creatures are programmed to avoid until all hope is gone, or self-sacrifice is required. From the very beginning of our life journey we have survival at the top of our agenda much of the time. The strange thing is, how rarely we appreciate having achieved this incredible goal every minute of every day. Nor do we stop to relish this 'being alive' because we learn to focus on what is next, rather than now or what we already have. To get the most out of life, we need occasional reminding of our most marvellous accomplishment.

Apart from society constantly showing us what else we could acquire, our strong natural survival mechanisms push us to compare and 'improve'. When these factors frequently occupy our minds things can get tiresome. Continual striving isn't much fun and it conceals the worth of what surrounds us. Everything becomes a means to some elusive end, and combating this is hard unless something changes.

Then we have an illness, an accident or a loss, and grasp how much we were overlooking as we stumbled through life. If we suffer a bereavement, suddenly we feel very sad and eventually very fortunate just to be here. Those we mourn can no longer enjoy everyday things like the sunlight, birds, flowers, a warm smile or a child's enthusiasm. Even regular inconveniences can be freshly savoured for the precious 'living' they involve. We regret not recognising or demonstrating how much we valued those who are no longer around, and hopefully this encourages us to express our positive feelings more freely in future.

If we are to cherish life, it helps to be reminded when we are taking it for granted. A loss can be our most potent nudge. An ordinary existence can transform into 'A Wonderful Life' when it's fragility is highlighted.

When we're wrapped up in day to day living we miss so much. It's a pity it often takes something as sad as a death to remind us how lucky we are just to wake up in the morning.

FOUND Out

It's been tough and rewarding trying to convey some of the lessons I learned. Tough because I've been pointing towards several realisations that are somewhat intuitive; rewarding because it has helped to clarify my thoughts and indicate areas for you to explore when you're ready. Thankfully the hardest part is over for me now, so it's on to the next adventure and I can't wait. On to –

The infinite world that makes people,
rather than the limited world people make.

The more open waters we have just passed through are nothing compared to the expanses of uncertainty that lie ahead. There childish notions have an essential expiry date and our small craft could drift anywhere. Nonetheless, a compelling enthusiasm urges us onward. If you want to come along I'll gladly show you around.

Join me there…

UNDISCOVERED

At last we've reached the ambitious latter stages of our tour, where perplexing mysteries abound.

Knowing

At this juncture there is one key insight we should take on board to help unlock our chains. It is – no matter what we have come to believe, in absolute terms we humans don't really *know* anything, and that includes me! In fact, you can disregard everything I'm writing due to my comprehension limitations. Yes, it has taken me a lifetime to learn, years to write, and it is almost certainly flawed. I'm sorry to have wasted so much of your valuable time... or have I?

Confused? Of course we are, and things just get more confusing from here on.

Not knowing, as a fundamental premise for life, is fascinating and liberating.

So what have all these clever folk we read about been up to for centuries? Essentially, doing their best. That's what people generally do. If we enjoy something or feel a need, and opportunities arise to pursue it, we will likely take them. The problems arise when we ignore, or fail to acknowledge, human limitations.

Remember, our pack instincts and childhood predispose us to looking up, individually and en-mass, to anything or anyone apparently superior. Then, those we rely on to 'know' often begin to believe they *do*, especially after any modicum of recognition. Specialists baffle us with their elaborate theories of multiple universes or black holes, which come across as places we might take a peek at sometime in the not too distant future, rather than the complex hypotheses they actually are. Those who profess to 'know', may not be deluding themselves but they seem to have most of *us* falling into line with their notions and interpretations. How odd, to find out all these smart Alecs aren't any brighter than the rest of us after all.

Er, well... they usually *are* much brighter, in their specialised fields at least. Our lives have been assisted markedly by Science, which requires substantial specialised brain power (and a lot of hard slog, graced with a fair slice of luck). That is by no means the full picture though. The thing is, specialists are steeped in what they do, so can understandably become blinkered. Fresh perspectives from elsewhere are advantageous, as is bearing in mind our capacity, or should I say lack of it, for comprehensive understanding.

I'm stating the obvious here because it doesn't appear that obvious to many of us. 'Knowing' means only what we can deduce. The basis of 'knowing' is what a select few temporarily agree on and the rest fall into line with. Our only means to 'know' are our minds and senses (albeit augmented by tools), and we are already partly aware of *their* considerable restrictions and distortions. When we add our concerns, preferences, presumptions, authorities and set approaches to the mix, the potential for misreckoning and tunnel vision is evident. What about the so called 'Flat Earth'? Then we had, 'The Solar System revolving around Earth' rather than the Sun. Or the age of the Earth before Rutherford came along to add several billion years. Repeatedly, some of the most respected and eminent experts are 'proved' to be wrong. It was not possible for our predecessors to comprehend what we can, just as it is not possible for us to comprehend or even theorise on what contradictory discoveries might turn out to be indisputably clear in future… well, clear for a while anyway.

This doesn't mean we shouldn't work with our theories. We certainly should. It's exploring, and that's a major feature of what we are. It plays an important part in our progress. Nevertheless, our faculties were primarily formed for survival and reproduction in particular environments, with all else taking care of itself. Understandably we want to do better, even if our sensory and comprehension apparatus was not exactly engineered for the acrobatics we have in mind.

Thousands of years ago our wise ancestors pointed out –

'To know, is to know we don't know.'

All we do is take the next step in our multi-directional journey, which can involve rejecting what enabled us to take every previous step. In this context, the conviction that often accompanies our latest theories, from those who should know better, seems most peculiar. At least they don't lack enthusiasm. *The fallibility of 'experts' may feel disconcerting to anyone with strong authority influences, as these can invoke an affiliation to established attitudes. A firm resistance to questioning widely held beliefs suggests deep-seated early conditioning factors are at work. Facing up to these is an important step on the road to freedom, growth and contentment.*

The wonderful thing about not knowing is that it lifts so much pressure. It frees us from pretensions, tradition and tired outlooks. Sure we can play the game for now, as long as we note events are constantly unfolding. This awareness takes us to another level of empowerment. Here we don't have to know all or any of the answers to participate, because no-one really does. All Science, Art, Literature, Mathematics or any other discipline is just a temporary construct by humans, of what seems to work for us at this point. It could be demolished forever or rebuilt at any time. Like a dead language, everything will inevitably be superseded. All our accolades and distinctions are merely humans recognising how capable some are in current fields. Who knows what we would be experiencing and appreciating now if we had chosen other paths centuries ago.

We each adopt our individual philosophies on how to deal with life every day. Seeing this as an open landscape we can all contribute to improving is far more constructive than a resigned deference that keeps us reliant and restricted. As someone once said about the untapped potential of every industrial workforce –

'With every pair of hands we get a free brain.'

…and that's only the beginning.

Super Science?

A reliance on Science has other implications besides continual reappraisal and superseding discoveries. As a discipline it is based on reason and evidence. That's fair enough, perhaps?

Why perhaps?

Because, in addition to the boundaries of human comprehension, there is a more subtle complication. Without looking too far, a significant omission is apparent – feelings. Humans are emotional beings chiefly, which most Science attempts to 'see past for our benefit' (except where emotions themselves are being studied, obviously). However it's not quite that straightforward, and valid questions come to mind. Firstly, what type and degree of emotional input *is* prevalent in Science? Secondly, will these attitudes tend to pursue or avoid particular considerations? Thirdly, and most importantly, indications are that our brains use logic, emotions and an array of other factors together in complex ways we don't understand. Overemphasis on certain aspects at the expense of others possibly reduces the effectiveness of the mix. How does this relate to Science and it's consequent likelihood of supplying fitting routes for balanced progress?

Meanwhile big changes to all our lives are in the pipeline, thanks to Science.

Our 'growing' ability to create compatible replacement limbs, tissue, organs and whatever body parts we require, opens a wealth of possibilities.

We can now fertilise and incubate human eggs and embryos artificially, to a large extent. When this can be done completely, changes to our sexuality will doubtless follow, creating interesting quandaries and very changed personal priorities.

Computerisation is in it's infancy. Currently it can be overwhelming due to it's many drawbacks including laborious programming, security weaknesses, demanding interfaces, ever-changing differing systems, compatibility and integration issues. Continuing exponential strides are imminent that should minimise our input while maximising their usefulness, freeing us to work on more enriching tasks.

Intelligent self-learning robot assistance is the next step. The question is where, if anywhere, will our emotional bias fit into the robotic 'efficiency' picture?

Like commercial technology, I expect selected scientific innovations are held in abeyance and unveiled only when the time seems right. Too much too soon could arouse social unrest. Current progress is liable to be more advanced than we appreciate, or need to.

Broader Horizons

Science is also venturing into less conventional territory. For example, inexplicable occurrences have been noted in the field of Quantum Mechanics. (The apparently miraculous observation of light particles that appear to be in more than one place at a time is now fairly common knowledge.) Seemingly no one fully understands the Quantum world, and they say anyone who claims to do so is demonstrating they don't. Even so, amazing breakthroughs presently being examined, based on Quantum and other Sciences, should transform our future dramatically. These include –

Flexible matter that can be moved remotely to replace using people e.g. in hazardous situations.

'Cloaks' that aim to create invisibility (yes just like the comic books).

Configuring atoms to construct the commodities we need (and probably much of what we don't) at the touch of a few buttons.

Developing instantaneous transportation by recreating precise atomic structure copies of anything, including people, in other locations.

Time and ethics permitting, experiments like these could have an unimaginable effect on our lives. As a popular Science Fiction character once said, 'It's life, but not as we know it.'

Space, Time & Other Mysteries

Our concepts of space and time were created by humans and are useful in day to day living. On closer examination we struggle to make sense of them for reasons that are debatable. Elaborate theories abound, all with similar limitations – us, our senses and our brains again. We can only observe, interpret and explain using the apparatus we have.

Where size and space are concerned, we've no idea how far up, down, out or round they go. At least we know we don't know. Discoveries indicate that different factors come into play at macro and micro levels; another aspect we have difficulty reconciling.

Testing Time

We regard time as a line – past, present and future; probably because that is how everything appears to us, like – yesterday, today, tomorrow; or birth, life, then death. By applying such a time line, the way I see it is – if the future is infinite (as widely believed) then we can't exist. Why? Because, taking the line view, the past would also be infinite so how could anything have come through it to be here now? Specialist theories propose sudden 'beginnings' of time as we know it, space/time connections, and time curves that involve travelling forward and meeting ourselves coming back (sort of). Maybe these will lead to something but, like all human concepts, there is surely much more to it.

What other inspired options could there be?

Obviously I have to hazard considered guesses, as anyone could, but here goes. From stories of consistently accurate predictions, psychics, reincarnation tales, converging coincidences and a degree of intuition, I am inclined to suggest that what we term 'the present' may be a conglomerate of what we consider to be the past, present and future. Not exactly 'Back To The Future' (that's another time line), more ever present while seeming to be separate. This is tricky stuff that feels almost ok to me, if not quite within our grasp, and I'm not the first to mention it (I have since learned).

Returning to our standard outlook for a moment, I say repeatedly we don't make the most of the present because our minds are preoccupied with the past and future, nevertheless the present isn't the full picture. The past is part of us, even if we only include our memories. Going further, reincarnation concepts may appeal predominantly to those who find death or loss hard to bear however, reports imply that some of us *can* occasionally access memories or effects from many years before our birth. My next ambitious suggestion would be to tie this in with our make-up…

If we pass-on useful characteristics or features from the past through our DNA or whatever, then some sort of extended capacity to access longstanding knowledge would significantly enhance the package. (After all, we hear most of our *current* life experiences appear to be somehow locked in our brains, if hardly ever consciously retrieved.) Automatically inheriting relatively low benefit aspects from our distant ancestors, like facial similarities, might make more sense if it is merely part of a blanket process that incorporates their arguably more helpful *experiences*, albeit by means we have still to establish. Beyond this, tracing all life back to a single cell with mechanisms to diversify while passing-on data could partly account for wider connections among various, if not all, life forms. Again this is another human straight-line model, only likely to reveal part of the picture.

We can barely begin to fathom the many mysteries of time and their implications. They combine with a plethora of puzzles from elsewhere to create considerable uncertainty. So if you were worrying that you might not actually have been an Egyptian Pharaoh after all (among the more popular and glamorous past life claims), hang on in there, nobody knows for sure. As long as you keep attending the therapist things should be fine.

Whatever Next?

We extend what we can see immensely using telescopes and microscopes, accepting they too have their limitations. Slow motion and time-lapse filming expose events and processes more fully than our unassisted observations allow. Using receivers we detect ultraviolet, infrared, electromagnetic fields, radio waves and numerous other activities around us that would otherwise be concealed. How much more could there be we haven't yet uncovered?

Outside the already detected presumably lies much that impacts on our lives we are only starting to consider. As we do, puzzles are 'solved' and new conundrums arise. Far from making us more sure of ourselves, increasing knowledge leads to ever more questions. Uncertainty turns up everywhere if sufficient questions are asked. Then we run into the limits of our imagination, which dictate what we examine next.

Infinite possibilities in an infinite number of directions may scare some but it is about as close as we get to 'real' for now, and offers exciting challenges for those intrepid enough to venture forward with trailblazing enthusiasm.

Connections & Coincidences

One of our most life enhancing capabilities is an open mind. Time now to really put this to the test.

Many of us have turned on the radio only to hear a song that was running through our head, or answered the phone to find someone we have been thinking about on the other end. When we cast our mind back, people and opportunities possibly appeared at the right times in our life, or is that just speculation? If you mention coincidences to folk, they often have their own stories to tell. Coincidences seem to occur and disappear from notice, leaving little trace in our distracted lives.

In an experiment involving adult male triplets, each was placed in a separate room and one was given minor shocks or similar. Even though the untreated pair felt nothing, scientists measured clear responses in both of them each time their brother was affected. This indicates they are connected in more ways than we recognise.

In another area, scientists have discovered correlations between (something like) – prime number distribution, vibration frequencies of metal bearings striking a glass ball, bus arrivals in a Mexican town, and parking patterns in parts of London. (The details aren't important for our purposes). Set number systems recur throughout Nature without us knowing why, entirely.

Accounts of unexplained coincidences and connections flow from a variety of reputable sources, as well as sceptics like me. Here's just *one* of mine...

I had been on holiday in March 2010 and stopped briefly in Whithorn. There I came across St Ninian's Museum (apparently he was one of the first Christians in Scotland). I felt noticeably at ease standing alone at dusk beside the ruins of his church. So much so, the memory lingered with me.

Later, during early summer, a woman stopped me as I was leaving a bar. As this rarely happens (in that way at least), I was curious. Although she said she was a nursery nurse, I remarked that she maybe had something to tell me. Sure enough, within a few minutes, she admitted to having psychic interests and told me about Newton's Cradle being linked with my work. Unbeknown to her, I had just written the early chapters of this book referring to it. A week later she sent me pictures from the Star Pyramid at Stirling Castle (she lived many miles from there), mentioning I would perhaps find it interesting. Stirling has been very significant in my life yet I knew nothing of this Pyramid. I let it pass, believing any relevance would unfold. After a few days, the woman contacted me again suggesting I should visit the Pyramid and I eventually agreed.

The night before my visit I was called by a friend I have known for fifteen years who I don't hear from often. I told her I was going to the Pyramid and that there could be a connection with St Ninian as I had just remembered St Ninian's is the big roundabout at Stirling. She laughed and told me her uncle used to be the curator of St Ninian's Museum in Whithorn. Lots of her childhood was spent playing at the ruins I had visited in March. This was the first time she had ever mentioned it, on the very night before my recommended visit to Stirling.

Next day I went to see the Pyramid. It was unusual because there were carved open bibles on all sides with three words on each page and references to the Psalms underneath. Nothing clicked till I went home and my mind settled. The words on the bibles were – Light and Truth; Word of God; Book of Life. I was writing my 'Book of Life', was this a coincidence?

Still, what about the Psalms? I checked the specific references and couldn't see anything obvious. (Connections are usually obvious; often so obvious we miss them.) The next week an unusual leaflet came through my door advertising a rare bible exhibition in my local library. The picture on the front was an open bible resembling those on the Pyramid. Was this significant? Was I missing something? I popped into the exhibition but left none the wiser.

A week or two later, for some reason I went to the studio where I had recorded my 'Love & Happiness' album from 2007 to 2009. When asked what I intended to do with the album, I said I was waiting to see how my Book turned out first. Both seemed linked somehow. When I mentioned the Pyramid and unresolved Psalms references, Ted at the studio enthusiastically forwarded a web link on the Psalms for me to peruse when I got home. I did, and they were all about praising Jehovah or other biblical stuff which didn't register with me.

Then the penny dropped…

The Psalms are all SONGS!

I checked the internet and it said something like, 'Psalms – from the Greek meaning, songs played/written on a stringed instrument.' I had written/played all the songs from my album on guitar; and Sandy, who produced it, is half Greek.

Songs at the bottom with the Book of Life above. This Pyramid I was directed to reflected what I was doing in ascending order, or so it appeared.

The following week I told this tale in the office. My pal, who recently came back to work with me following twenty five years apart, happened to be around when I was telling the story. He jumped to his feet and rushed out claiming it was a very strange coincidence. Soon he returned with his phone. On the screensaver was a photo of… guess what? Yes, the Star Pyramid in Stirling! He had been to this obscure monument two weeks after me for no particular reason, and just decided to put it on the front of his phone. The Pyramid is far from anywhere he would normally be.

That's not the full story, but it's enough.

Coincidences? Perhaps.

Granted our brains want to make sense of things, and they do come up with highly creative explanations from time to time. That said, I'm keeping an open mind.

The Abstract & Metaphysical

There are numerous accounts of 'out of body' experiences and extremely peculiar events. I've had a few extraordinary episodes of my own. I have also met reliable people who say they encounter (non-alcoholic) 'spirit' presences. If the abundant claims are anything to go by, I expect this is just scratching the surface. In short, reports suggest that with a bit more exploration in the right places we could discover astonishing things.

Historical cultures contain a diverse range of beliefs and techniques, some of which continue to exist on the edges of our modern, so called, reality. This is where we find bold concepts. Less shackled by convention, they treat us to a wealth of possibilities. Different existence dimensions; inner body pathways to deeper 'energy' presences; our life sources beyond the physical and much more. These have been unfolding as far back as we can trace and are still startling to the unprepared.

As Science progresses and our minds open we are starting to consider that previously discounted claims may contain a modicum of validity, at the very least. Admittedly many dubious tales do arise. These are the inevitable by-products of any open-minded outlook. They can be far more easily dismissed than the unhappiness, ill-health and conflict our current limited mainstream produces. Is their susceptibility to ridicule why we haven't derived much, if any, of their value?

Strange Benefactors

If we imagine our understanding process as a series of concentric circles, we should probably begin at the centre and move steadily outwards as we learn. However, some of us rush through, or skip past, circles while most of us prefer to stick to the circles we know (oblivious to this image of course). Those in the outer circles may be pioneers or crazy or both. They are likely to have bypassed several stages. Some might not be deemed 'normal', which allows them more latitude for expression. They could be rude, self-centred, uncomfortable with people, lacking in common sense, or unable to handle their own affairs. Philosophers, boffins, dropouts, or anyone widely regarded as very unusual, or with curious talents, might qualify. Not fitting the mould means they operate outwith it, often appearing to make great personal sacrifices. Perhaps they are isolated, choosing to live apart in order to do their thing. They may be tormented and on the verge of madness, slipping in and out of accepted sanity, testing their unorthodox paths. The grounded majority prefer a more standard approach, remaining sceptical or threatened by the unconventional. This is how we miss out. Humans come with a wealth of remarkable innovative resources, regularly misread or spurned due to surface impressions and fears associated with their failure to comply with what we regard as normality.

Warning Signs

There is, predictably, a critical hitch with certain avant-garde perspectives. In the case of abstract concepts, just as elsewhere, the notion that humans can describe or even sense anything approaching total comprehension is somewhat overambitious. Unfortunately, many profound explorations of 'truth' fail to recognise that any truth we expound or experience, no matter how abstract, is merely a human interpretation. I'm not insinuating every attempted revelation is unfounded. My point is, we don't know. All I *can* say is – coming via humans, even when they are supposed to be searching outwith human constraints, abstract concepts are just *people's* explanations. They are very unlikely to tell the whole story... if there is one?

Fretting about acknowledgment of ideas and views is another indicator of questionable perception. Appreciating our best efforts is valid, requiring others to do so is a cry for recognition. Theories about life amount to little more than self-expression, albeit well-intentioned. Anyone who can begin to envisage the extent of mystery behind everything is liable to be reflecting in awe at their good fortune just to be present. True Sages are more interested in enjoying the astounding fluke of being alive with the enrichment it entails, than glory hunting.

Mind Over Matters

Despite the detours, abstract themes offer approaches outside conventional reason that can expand our horizons profitably. How? One way is by considering the possibility that thoughts play a far bigger part in shaping our lives than most of us would imagine –

*'A man happily observed a religious fast for days on end.
His neighbour starved to death on the same diet.'*

The power of the mind is indisputable. (Recently we have created interfaces that use brain activity alone to operate electronic devices remotely.) Our thinking affects how we feel and it can have a considerable influence on our circumstances. Teachings on positive and negative thinking permeate much of our achievement culture, with Business, Life and Sports Coaches assuring us of their power. Furthermore, *expectations* alter our responses – placebos can produce 30 to 40 percent success rates, and 'faith healing' (probably similarly based on belief) can deliver surprising successes. The mind-created physical effects of psychosomatic illness are all too real for the sufferers, and some surgical procedures can now be performed under hypnosis alone. Lying on beds of nails, walking on hot coals, or breaking bricks with our bare hands may not be for the faint hearted but, given sufficient practice, they are sometimes possible without too much damage if we achieve an appropriate mindset.

Everything appears to be tied to, if not totally produced by, our mind. Most experiences come via our brain which means we only know what may be real or otherwise when our brain tells us, and it is a master manipulator. So how do we know what *is* real? Clearly, we don't! Nothing at all might exist. Our dreams could be reality and what we think of as awake could be sleep. Everything and everyone could be a mirage, a mind construct. How would we know? (This recognition comes precariously close to the edge of our current consideration limits, mine anyway.)

Ancient writings from around the globe imply we can be in more than one place at a time – yes, like the light particles I mentioned earlier. They also suggest we can move through time, and think of situations or people which then appear.

Some propose we can levitate and pass through solid objects when conducive states of mind are achieved. Is anything possible? Maybe a form of consciousness, as we call it, is a reality beyond the physical with the power to create and modify at will when we learn to suitably engage it. Is that what we are already doing, obliviously?

'So what? This sounds crazy!' you say. Crazy perhaps, but it beats showbiz gossip and hype… for a while.

Who's to say what lies dormant within and among us. Are we marking time or, even worse, going backwards when we could be forging ahead? Is there an abundance of pathways we can barely contemplate just waiting to be travelled and appreciated? We don't know and we *won't* know if we keep thinking what we notice, and extensions of it, is all we can experience and utilise.

How many reasons do we need to wisely examine what we can, abstract or otherwise, when there are so many of us ready for more fitting and fulfilling lives?

People

People are fascinating, and they're everywhere aren't they. Mmm… no, not exactly. Our heads might be full of people paraphernalia but a cursory glance, even in a busy city street, reveals that most of the space around us is occupied by other things. Buildings, traffic, roads, pavements, sky and air occupy most of our urban settings. Animals, plants, open land, sea, birds and insects lie beyond. That's before we consider outer-space, which has very few people as far as I can tell. People account for a tiny proportion of our surroundings, yet we continually concern ourselves with them and their view of us. (Meanwhile we forget they are likewise almost totally absorbed with their own place among others and how *they* are being perceived.) This understandable people preoccupation limits our vision. We look at ourselves and the world through other people, as if standing in a human circle facing inwards. People are always the largest part of the picture. If we turn to face outwards (metaphorically speaking), our perspective opens up tremendously. People are still around, without always dominating the scene.

Among other things, this change enables us to gain helpful insights by seeing people in broader terms –

1. As a species.
2. As processing.
3. As energy.
4. As stuff that combines in a certain way to make things we call people.

Being Humans

We are relatively capable separate individuals who come together to cooperate. This includes breeding, defence, support, stimulation, sharing, and progress enhancement. Individuality enables flexible combinations and valuable diversity. As time passes, individuals come and go while the species develops or deteriorates. That's part of the story.

Problematic Processors

Like most life forms we take in a range of things, such as water, air and information; process them; then use much of what they produce e.g. energy and solutions, to get by. Crucially, various aspects in and around us act on the human processor's ability to flow readily or not, affecting our satisfactory operation. Toxic fumes and chemicals harm our bodies, that is clear enough. What isn't so clear is the kind of exposure that strains our emotions, and it's serious repercussions. Our minds and bodies work in harmony, so they alert each other. *Physical* ill health can be a warning against damaging *mental* influences, as much as taste, smell and appearance caution us against consuming dangerous food.

I hadn't visited the doctor for several years before an exceptionally emotional relationship. During the two years it lasted I acquired assorted infections, all of which subsided not long after the relationship ended. That is not to say the other person was responsible. No, my undetected vulnerabilities led to the damage. How much physical illness is being caused by inappropriate contact? The warning signs are usually clear when we learn how to spot them.

Recent research shows swearing is connected to negativity in the brain and, despite my too frequent indulgences, I now sense a dragging down effect from 'bad' language and am inclined to minimise my involvement. Likewise, I tend to automatically recoil and withdraw from loud forceful people, sensing the agitation they create in me. Frequent complainers, arguers and criticisers also activate my protective 'see you later' mechanisms. I now realise that I feel much better and calmer away from negativity (including my own), most of us do.

Finding The Energy

Humans generate and consume energy continuously to varying extents, how we use and replenish it is key. Things feel more taxing when we are tired, our resourcefulness diminishes and we can become ill. Adequate rest and breaks reduce strain and improve performance. Emotional and physical ailments often heal faster given plenty of rest. It can take months or years to recharge energy levels after a crisis. In extreme cases they may never totally recover, which can show in recurring illness and/or lost enthusiasm.

Excessive thinking, typically tied in with our fears, is a noteworthy energy thief that can induce a raft of unforeseen ailments. (Apparently brains account for only two percent of our body mass whereas they consume twenty percent of our energy.)

In the wider picture, it seems 'energy' that can be picked up by other creatures emanates from us. Our understanding of this is rudimentary; there could be numerous types of subtle 'energies' being projected and received. Personal auras, attraction and intuitions might be linked to energy transmitting and receiving. Not wishing to confuse Science with speculation, all I will say is – our bodies are energy processors so don't be too surprised if we discover 'energy' flows that affect us more than we *currently* recognise.

The Stuff Of Life

As far as we can tell, humans are a coincidental combination of fairly standard substances and electrical impulses mixed in a precise way over time. (I did say, 'As far as we can tell.') Intriguingly, all formations have aspects of this in common. Not only life forms but also mountains, stars, gases and everything on the physical level at least. So, add a tweak of fate, a dollop of time, and hey presto!… inconceivable permutations with diverse features could emerge – from the inanimate to consciousness may be less of an issue than we suppose, and it doesn't stop there. Throughout life and beyond, the chemicals and energy our bodies consist of are continually being exchanged with their surroundings. This could imply more intrinsic connections across the board. If our world starts and ends with people, perhaps we should reconsider.

There is no scarcity of more immediate discovering to do. In the last few years, ocean explorers have found a loosely put together 'living' entity full of gaps, about the size and shape of a party balloon. It consists of bits and pieces we can knock apart with a few swipes. Moments after being dispersed, it reassembles and resumes pulsating gently as before. If this isn't a hoax, it looks like established lines between life and environment have already blurred, if not disappeared.

A Matter Of Life Or Death

Basking in the increased light of human understanding limitations and associated infinite possibilities, it is now worth reflecting on our ideas about death.

Let's face it, death has a poor image. It's lack of appeal is universal in all but the most desperate (or deluded) circumstances. Having said that, nobody has gone and reported back so there isn't any concrete information or reviews to base our expectations on. Undoubtedly, bereavement is a very sad process to endure, few would dispute that. Death, on the other hand, is a complete unknown. Maybe, if we strip away our conventional taboos about death, we might find something curiously comforting and liberating. Without brain function we don't experience anything, as far as we know. When our brain stops working it's over for us. Nothing to deal with, no bills to pay, no health worries, no sales calls, nothing. It comes to us all. We can't have life without death so why all the fuss? Imagine that attitude being widespread. The threat and drama of death, that permeates and impedes much of our existence, losing it's stranglehold.

Fear Fool

Preferring to be alive rather than dead would seem vital for any conscious type of life to persist. Sadly though, some humans are prone to a preoccupation with this kind of concern. Once again our frantic projecting minds are trying to deal with an unfathomable future, and failing spectacularly. Taking us away from what is happening now, to consider an event that we essentially never have to experience, is surely masochistic madness. As Julius Caesar apparently stated, rather harshly –

'Brave men die once, cowards die many times.'

Worrying about dying prevents us from living, demonstrating again how fear repeatedly exerts a power beyond it's justification. (I'm not talking about the specific painful fear of death caused by a medical diagnosis or sentence of execution. That is unquestionably traumatic.)

A persistent fear of death and it's consequences, fuelled by a mindset or belief system, is liable to be like many recurring fears – representative of something else. As death is an unknown, our fears are possibly tying it in with earlier encounters we disliked considerably. Darkness, solitude, abandonment, loss, and powerlessness are some likely candidates.

Doctrines On Death

Understandably, death captures our imagination. Since before civilisations began, theories on death have occupied the thoughts of those fortunate enough to have had the luxury of contemplation time. From Pharaohs, who spent much of their *actual* life building elaborate tombs for the 'next life', to philosophical and religious scholars offering their more gainfully employed followers convenient interpretations of what lies beyond, there has been a profusion of speculation. People regularly take this conjecture at face value and alas, not only are theories of 'where we go' when we die speculative, they can also be oppressive.

Death is an impenetrable mystery. (That's presumably why our close personal losses can be impossible to absorb, and why trying to understand them makes matters worse.) Comprehension of the 'unknowable' is a contradiction best respected. It's too steep a mountain to climb, that draws the desperate and unsuspecting at their peril.

Reassessing

Contemplating death is not an *entirely* pointless pursuit. It is undeniably significant, so a measure of reflection won't go amiss.

Considering our view of death starts with a better appreciation of life and the phenomenon it is, when we grasp the super-slim chance of us ever existing in the first place. We search for miracles, while in the vastness of time and space there are few possibilities so remote as us.

Then we might mull over factors such as –

1. Our ideas of time being a line (or anything else).

2. What defines existence? We are only aware of existence states we can detect. What else is there?

3. Our state of mind and emotions often drive our other apparatus, so how do they affect what existences we perceive or fail to?

4. Conditioned thinking and stifled functioning could be clouding our vision.

5. What about so called 'spirits', 'life forces' or 'energies'?

*6. To what extent and in what way is anything a part
of every other thing throughout time, space and
undiscovered zones?*

It soon becomes clear that Rocket Science is mere child's play compared to fully reconciling our ideas of life and death. So much so, that the fallback conventional view is necessary for most of us, if only to avoid a complete mental meltdown. What I'm saying is that there are countless unknowns when it comes to death. From reincarnation to non-existence, anything is possible. We can only choose what view works for us at the time, allowing for the distinct possibility that it is probably more expedient than complete. Realising human ideas of life and death are no more than our perspective, and likely to be a simplification at best, encourages a progressive openness to other considerations as we develop, without diminishing our respect for life in any regard.

Dead Or Alive?

A death we know more about is the living kind. People give up their lives for what they believe. If you think that's extreme, think again. We all give up our life for what we believe in – security, success, money, popularity, searching, whatever. Every life is given up to what it involves without most of us seeing it that way. Is this a waste? A better question might be – are we making the most of life? Our friends, families, work, interests and aptitudes all present opportunities and rewards but do we embrace them? Are they enough; and if not, why not?

Understanding our life choices is pivotal. Whether we conform or rebel, it is worth considering if obsolete engrained tactics for 'survival' or obtaining recognition predispose us to a life of self-sacrifice or inertia. Have childhood fears and reinforcing exposure dictated our opt in or opt out decisions? Are we judiciously employing our bespoke up to the minute discernment to direct our life, or the straightjacketing interpretations of others? Have we grown up yet, sufficiently examined our make-up and tried our own approaches?

Until we learn to figure out what underlies our emotions, and think independently (to whatever extent that is possible), we remain pawns in someone else's game, depriving ourselves and humanity of our unique contribution. Exposing and questioning the influences we take for granted could prevent us from squandering our most precious gift, and open doors to a far more fulfilling existence. Are we willing to assume our responsibility for enhancing life here and now, rather than living in fatalistic acceptance or the hope there could be a 'big lottery win' waiting for us in another time, another place? After all, why not make the most of what we have now *in addition to* any other future prospects? One way or another we all choose, and experience life accordingly.

UNDISCOVERED Uncovered

Latterly I've alluded to realms that lie beyond human comprehension. This sounds somewhat contradictory so it would be no mean feat to dip into them, and there could be a way.

Till now we have used our minds like ships to briefly tour relevant topics. The next stage is to use them like *spaceships*, to escape the gravity pull of constant thinking – use our minds to escape our minds, so to speak. No, wait! Don't run, it's not quite as mad as it sounds.

A trauma, enough discontent or a book like this might provide the initial blast needed. Then, by learning how to rest our thoughts, we can 'float out' into uncharted territory where connected feelings produce an acceptance that far surpasses our reasoning. There is infinitely more out there (or in there) than we're prepared for. All we can do is learn to vacate our mind-dominated atmosphere for a time and enable ourselves to glimpse this vast, peaceful, unfamiliar environment. How do we get there? Simple. I said simple, not easy. Reducing our mental activity for periods is the key. It takes some work, patience and time. Not seeking or responding to distractions is incredibly taxing at first. Gradually, by minimising external stimulation and watching how we respond, calmer feelings arise. When our barriers of mind noise subside, a warm tide of contentment flows in.

Returning to our thought-based world from this place brings new energy, freedom and a wealth of fresh perspectives, making regular journeys like these an important part of our completeness. Yes I mentioned this earlier but now, having glimpsed the amount of undiscovered territory out there, transcending our standard paths takes on an even greater significance.

HANDOVER

It's almost time to embark on your own adventures now. Before you do, here are a few final factors to ease your passage…

Where To Now?

Aah, the future. A topic I have brought into question on several counts. It would be easy to avoid by invoking my doubts again although, after careful consideration, I've decided it's far too interesting for that cop-out. So, setting aside possible cataclysmic events for the time being, let's take another under-equipped human peek down this highly unlikely time tunnel to see where it might lead.

In the relatively short term, continuing to build on superficial attitudes and approaches will create ever more narrow, homogenised, teetering lives, prone to toppling at the slightest nudge. The more entwined our precariously founded groupings become, in order to prop up this house of cards, the greater the domino effect of any collapse is likely to be (excuse the mixed metaphors).

Alternatively, if we learn to make adequately informed choices by exploding widely held myths and recognising our part in a realistic bigger picture, we will consume, and consequently create, less rubbish. Counterproductive nonsense will also reduce while more satisfying and efficient work, better suited to our aptitudes, should emerge. Essentially, our lives would be greatly enhanced.

It's worth bearing in mind that positive change seems to flow from improved understanding, and it gathers it's own momentum. Forcing is rarely the best option. Too much change too soon is too risky. A soft landing where possible is always preferable to crash and burn.

Looking further is enormously speculative though truly fascinating. Conventional theories suggest what might remain long after 'everything' is gone – 'Photons forever,' is one typically uninspiring conclusion. In the meantime we will doubtless re-engineer our fragile organic bodies into more robust mechanisms. Thereafter, physical human functioning could eventually disappear, giving way to an entirely mental apparatus. (Of course, as I mentioned earlier, this may be what is happening already without us realising. A complication that doesn't really help us here.)

Full Circle

By being exceptionally creative we can come up with intriguing long-term future scenarios that actually help us *now*. This involves two things. The first is no great surprise i.e. acknowledging human reasoning limitations. The other entails projecting to the edges of our current imagination. These related factors can be combined to give surprising results.

What if we ignore all rational impediments to any possibilities by applying the first point. That is to say, by accepting that any apparent obstacles are merely based on human perception limitations and therefore bound to be surmountable by means we have simply yet to establish. Given this context, anything we can think of may be achievable in time.

Now we can really stretch our imaginations.

What if we could – live forever healthily and without threats; have anything we wanted; travel anywhere instantly; manipulate time to our wishes?

Hooray! No limits! This is what we are striving for, so what if we had it? Paradise! Sounds great doesn't it. Doesn't it? Well… once we get over the initial novelty of limitless power it begins to feel quite lacklustre, sterile even. Too easy, perhaps? Looks like we haven't really thought through this eagerly anticipated 'Utopia', with all it's idealised notions and promises of perfection.

Has our ambitious delve into every desirable future achievement confirmed what we least expected? That, no matter what dizzy heights we attain, life isn't only about that or it would be too bland. Life is an ever changing mixture of experiences whose relative nature is key to us. We are comparison machines painstakingly attuned over aeons to aim for what is 'preferable' and avoid what is not. In a world of perfection with nothing to achieve, what would we do? What would drive us? Already we have many problematic examples of complacent living which illustrate the dangers of demotivation. Whatever is accomplished, we are mostly shaped by and for suitable challenges with the relative 'gains or losses' they deliver and risks involved. Apart from occasional well earned breaks and indulgences, dealing with life's immediate requirements is where I can foresee most of our greatest gratifications being obtained, particularly when we manage to match tasks to our abilities.

Any otherwise 'artificially induced' form of lasting happiness is likely to upset our delicate organic equilibrium, be high maintenance and ultimately threatening to our existence as humans (albeit, in time, a hybrid species could be more resilient).

So much for the future with it's deceptive allure which, when traced to an adequate conclusion, kind of leads us back to our apt, if by no means faultless, set of circumstances in the present.

Our life *may* be about the journey, as much as any destination, after all.

The End Of The Beginning

We're rounding off our expedition now, returning to where it all began with extended vision. Here life's oceans meet our expanding shore, and I take my leave. It will be interesting to see what you choose to do (or allow to happen) next.

I haven't covered the full story though, not by any means. It's always unfolding. Everyone helps to write it every day in their own way. If I've done my job, you will recognise that the real journey is just starting. It's up to you to come up with your own questions, answers and connections.

My work isn't prescriptive, it's partly explanatory, primarily exploratory. I'm in the business of raising questions more than recommending answers, and helping people to help themselves. I have merely sown a few seeds that could bear fruit if you choose to nurture them. Personal choices play a huge part in determining the quality of our lives. Where we go and how far is probably a matter of priorities, perspective and potential.

The way we look at the world affects how we feel, and the more complete our view is the more complete our life is liable to be. When our view doesn't fit or we force a view to fit, we are susceptible to suffering unduly. Things may go ok for a while however, as soon as they get tough and our 'forced' views are threatened, despair or calamity often ensues. It can take this weight of pain to demand a rethink. If your outlook isn't working repeatedly, try broadening it. You may feel strange at first but the acid test is – given a proper chance, does the change fit better and deliver?

It's not really about agreeing or disagreeing or debate or arguments. The elaborate rationale we manage to concoct is usually a product of our programming. Normally a willingness to consider we might be missing key points goes against the grain, so most of the counter 'reasoning' we expound is produced by our underlying emotions attempting to justify, often inherited, entrenched positions using whatever tactics we can conjure up. Some of us are just slicker than average at these manoeuvres (or more determined). The question effectively boils down to – do we stick with the familiar, or admit our oversights, feel a bit foolish and start to look deeper within and without for improvements? Learn or suffer, these are the options. Given a little humility and the courage to at least consider our self-imposed impediments, there is more than a fair chance we will reap escalating returns.

Every minute is a new beginning with opportunities to find worthwhile ways. Ways to remove the acquired barriers that keep us trapped like insatiable munching caterpillars, rather than the bright butterflies Nature intends. If we mange to shake off old layers, our new wings will take us high above the undergrowth where everything becomes clearer and fresher. Then the colours and actions we spread can brighten our surroundings and put smiles on faces, frequently without us even knowing.

Individuals shape the world, and our individual contribution touches the world around us somehow. Waiting for something or someone else to act or change is a prison that overlooks our innate capacity to seek out viable options.

So there we are, it's up to you. The same old same old or an array of new avenues to explore? Perhaps it *won't* make much difference, except to you. To *you* it could make a world of difference.

Writing This Book

It's been a monumental endeavour. The biggest I've ever undertaken, voluntarily. I wanted to share my experiences for the benefit of others, and was able to invoke a longer-term mindset than I'm accustomed to, so I did it.

Writing is a solitary task, and the topic necessitated a level of sustained detachment I found unhealthy. Such an all-encompassing subject also requires a debilitating intensity of thought I would strongly warn against; far sharper minds than mine have buckled under the strain. Occasional forays are fine, any more is dangerous. The near constant thinking fed on itself, taking me away from the greater contentment I had gained and back to an agitated projecting mindset that eventually craved completion. The mental effort led to a range of physical ailments necessitating several months respite and a drastically reduced pace towards the end. Fortunately I was always aware sacrifices would be required and their mainly temporary, if not specific, nature. So I stuck with it, through thick and thin!

I'm glad I did it but right now I'm more glad it's over. Time will provide a truer assessment of the work. Did I make the right decision writing this? Of course I did, there was barely any deciding involved. Would I do it again? I couldn't... I'm learning my limits.

Summing Up

What? You expected a snappy ending? Something entertaining, concise and practical that encapsulates all I've been trying to say. Hmm… it's a tall order.

OK, there *is* a saying which pretty much sums up my view –

> *The world is perfect but there is a lot of room for improvement.*

Another good maxim is –

> *The only thing we need to be happy is something to be enthusiastic about.*

And Buddha provided some of the wisest words when he pointed out –

> *'This path leads to the highest happiness, and the highest happiness is peace.'*

Or what about the ultimate summary –

> *When the sage was asked to fit everything into a sentence, he said, 'I can do better than that. I can put it in a word – Silence.'*

These all offer very helpful messages, but there is one other that fits the bill exceptionally well…

Happy Ending

After all our adventures, one very important place hasn't even been mentioned. It is possibly the most important of all. That's why I saved it for last, you've earned it.

Recently I came across a clever little story which succinctly describes the milestones of my journey along with their lessons and a final key message. It slipped through the net numerous times before registering, which shows how easily we can overlook even the most relevant details until we're ready. Only now that our extensive tour is complete can it begin to deliver it's liberating insights with minimum misinterpretation.

This is what everything I've been taking great pains to convey amounts to. About as close as words can take us anyway –

When an acclaimed wise man was asked to explain his path to enlightenment and happiness, he answered, "God first led me by the hand into the Land of Action, and there I dwelt for several years. Then he returned and led me to the Land of Sorrows; there I lived until my heart was purged of every attachment. That is when I found myself in the Land of Love, whose burning flames consumed whatever was left in me of self. This brought me to the Land of Silence, where the mysteries of life and death were bared before my wondering eyes."

"Was that the final stage of your quest?" he was then asked. "Oh no," he replied. "One day God said, 'Today

I will take you to the innermost sanctuary of the temple, to the heart of God himself,' and I was led to the Land of Laughter."

Bon Voyage!